LETTERS FROM LOVE CAFÉ
First Series

MEMO OZDOGAN

Love is the only light.

Memo

"The joyful super genius secretly hidden in the pages of this book is like a spiritual bomb with a natural potential to trigger an earthquake of the highest magnitude possible which will shake the global spiritual, intellectual and philosophical community at its foundation. It surely is a simply wise, supremely intelligent, vitally rejuvenating and exquisitely dynamic masterpiece which is entirely different from the money making entertainment business that is going on currently in the name of so called new age spirituality. This book is a kind of majestic spiritual thunderstorm with a lightening which has the power to touch and transform the suffering souls of those who are lucky enough to recognize and distinguish the dancing light of the guiding star rising amidst appalling spiritual darkness of confusion in the world today. A very rare explosion of the love of truth at the highest mountain tops which will probably be the beginning of a new era of true spirituality and philosophy. Your heart will know the difference immediately, and your life can never be the same again after hearing the silent, wise and tender whispering of love through **The Blue Book**."

THE TEMPLE OF ILLUMINATION BOOK REVIEW

*"Neither a lofty degree of intelligence nor imagination
nor both together go to the making of genius.
Love, love, love, that is the soul of genius."*
Wolfgang Amadeus Mozart

"Truth is a pathless land."

Jiddu Krishnamurti

*"Religion is for people who're afraid of going to hell.
Spirituality is for those who've already been there."*
Vine Deloria Jr.

Foreword

It was around early 2012 when I was first inspired for the 'Letters from Love Café' series and over the course of two years I have authored 47 letters whenever the inspiration for that particular letter came unexpectedly the way the breeze comes in through an open window. The letters are about living itself in general, and in particular they include subjects such as spirituality, the path of happiness, living in the present, love, meditation and wisdom.

I decided to publish this first edition when the comings of the inspirations have stopped months ago together with a new and recent inspiration for a novel which appeared in the horizon with the name of 'Love of Sophia' as the second coming. Such inspirations when they come are like inevitable births. One is being forced in a way to materialize such visions of inspirations. Therefore, with the appearance of 'Love of Sophia', letters have come to an end, at least for now, to be published as the first edition though I do have a strong feeling that they will continue in a future edition whenever the inspiration comes again.

I do hope you will enjoy reading the letters, and I will sincerely be very happy if somehow they help you one way or another in your journey of life.

Memo Ozdogan

ABOUT THE AUTHOR

From his early twenties, Memo Ozdogan has had great passion and personal interest in exploring western and eastern philosophy in order to see and understand different approaches towards the subject of living. He has delved into modern psychology, the original teachings of the Buddha, J.Krishnamurti, Rumi, Ancient Greek philosophy, ancient forms of spirituality and new age spirituality.

After deeply studying all these various approaches, he tried to find out the original truth in each of these different approaches without becoming a static follower of any of them. He quotes: "life is a very dynamic and living thing which is ever-changing, and therefore no philosophy of the past can be applied directly to life which takes place in the present moment. Philosophy or teachings might point out an important truth and much can be learned from them but one should never get stuck at any of them since life must be explored from moment to moment and that means one must continue one's inner journey of discovery at this present moment. This is the only door opening to the path of true happiness and liberation".

Memo is currently a teacher at 'Find Your Secret Key' and 'The Temple of Illumination'.

www.facebook.com/FindYourSecretKey

THE SECRET KEY

The lone tree of the mountain tops whispered through silence;

"There is your beloved living in the kingdom of happiness
Dancing in bliss in the secret garden of love
What you begin to see is the door to this kingdom
What you should find is the secret key

Look for the beloved in the setting sun of far horizons
Search for her where the moon touches the waters
Get intoxicated with her smile shining through the stars
Smell her eternal beauty in the fresh morning breeze

Fall desperately in love with her and get lost
Rejoice in this love and dispel the darkness of fear
Let the light of joy touch the heart in this mad love
Free the all-consuming passion to light the fire
Listen to the song of the ecstatic unity

In that song lover becomes one with the beloved
Beloved then becomes life itself
And such love for her
The secret key..."

Memo Ozdogan

CONTENTS

Letter#23
November 29, 2012

Inward Nakedness

"You will feel your soul being undressed when the tender hands of love begin touching you. The many different masks on one's face will be removed, and the many different clothes which one is attached to will be ripped off one by one.

Then, there will be a feeling of nothingness inwardly. Nothing to hold on to, nothing to be attached to, and nothing to lose; therefore no fear. And, when you are so totally naked inwardly, there will be a feeling of innocence. This will be the beginning of your immortal love story with the beloved."
Memo Ozdogan

FIND YOUR SECRET KEY

Open the door to the light of joyful living

www.facebook.com/FindYourSecretKey
www.FindYourSecretKey.com

LETTERS FROM LOVE CAFÉ

Memo Ozdogan

Letter#1
May 1st. 2012

Meet your fear for a drink

Psychological fear of any kind is probably at the very heart of the origin of our misery and unhappiness because they darken life greatly. And it seems the only way we know to deal with it is to escape from it through many different means, never realizing the fact that as long as we run away from fear it will run after us like a dark shadow until we die. We can do all kinds of things to escape from the pain of fear, but fear will always be waiting for us in the loneliness of our homes when we come back from such escapes.

Can we stop all escapes totally for one time in our lives to meet fear face to face from a very close distance and look at it with full attention? And once we stop, will fear, which is like a dark shadow, stop running after us as well? What happens then? Now, for the first time we shall experience facing fear directly instead of escaping from it and therefore because we are able to face it directly we will be able to see and understand what fear is all about. This process can never be possible when we constantly try to escape from fear. And then, perhaps we will also discover how easy it is to face it.

What is there to fear then? When there was escape we were chased by fear, but once we stop and face fear, it will disappear. A friendly relationship with fear can take place only when we give our full attention, to listen to its story and understand it in the way we listen to our loved ones. Such loving attention will cure fear instantly, whereas escaping from it will sustain and give strength to it. There is no method of facing fear. All you need to do is to stop "escape" of any kind in all its subtle forms. The moment all such movement of escaping away from fear comes to an end, we are face to face with fear and that very moment of being face to face with it in the real sense is the ending of fear. Only then joy will naturally begin to take root in your life. The breeze of joy can never enter the house of fear with all its windows firmly shut.

So why don't you try a fundamentally new approach and meet fear for a drink "today" because "tomorrow" is another form of escape.

Delaying action is probably the worst among all fear, since allowing time to enter the equation is the most subtle trick of the mind, preventing immediate action. Immediate action is the only way to deal with fear. This is really a 'now or never" case.

Make an appointment "now" at "Love Café" and after having some wine and getting drunk, you will find yourself in great laughter, face to face with joy instead of fear, and joy will say to you: "I will be gone and fear will come back again when you are sober. If you want to meet me again, come to this café more often to face fear and to have some more of this wine. And there will come a time where you will begin to live in this café with me all the time, drunk with love, never getting sober again. And this unique smile on your face now, which is my mirror reflection, will be there all the time. "

Letter#2
May 9th. 2012

"Stop seeking happiness. As long as you seek it, it will never come to you. Just open the window of your heart and the breeze of joy will find its way."

The right path of true happiness
Happiness has been the central issue of philosophy, spirituality, psychology, religion, as well as for the ordinary human being from the beginning of mankind and this search is still going on today, since it clearly seems humanity cannot find an absolutely satisfying answer to this question of happiness. Though humanity has tried many different methods and formulas to attain such true happiness, it seems none of them have really worked because as we observe we can see humanity is getting more and more unhappy, and if any formula has worked everybody would be applying it but obviously there is no such one common formula that can applied to billions of human beings. For that reason instead of such general formulas for all, which obviously have never worked and will never work, one must start the search to find his or her "unique" secret key which will open the door to the light of joyful living. Such search implies deep river diving rather than swimming on the surface and this very diving

itself becomes the purpose and the meaning of life. The very first step towards such depths in this adventurous and joyful inner journey of discovery becomes the very last one, and at this point all seeking of happiness at any direction comes to an end. Then, at this very moment such joy might touch our souls unexpectedly with no invitation just like the breeze outside coming in whenever it will. But we must prepare our houses and open the window for the breeze to find its way in, and the very process of the search for our secret keys becomes the process of preparing our houses and opening the windows.

Happiness is neither to be purchased at a certain price nor can be captured by running after. Rather, it must come naturally like the breeze. If one seeks or runs after it one can never have it. One can get pleasure by seeking it, but pleasure is an entirely different feeling to happiness. What becomes important then is to stop seeking it, but at the same time one must prepare one's house and open the window for the breeze to come in.

Practical suggestions on happiness:
-Live rightly by keeping the physical body light and healthy.
-Always preserve a close relationship with nature since nature has the secret doctrine.
-Do natural yoga, such as, hiking in nature and swimming.
-Learn to listen to the voice of your heart and find a balance between the mind and the heart.
-Do your best in life but do not compare yourself with anybody inwardly.
-Do not accept the authority of experts on how to be happy because if they knew they themselves would be happy. And if they were happy they would not attempt to give you dead formulas of happiness. Anybody who has such formulas to offer others knows nothing about happiness. Find out for yourself as this is your journey and no expert can give you your "unique" secret key, which will open the door to a joyful life.
-Stay away from people or environments where your heart feels lack of love.
-Do not accept what society wants to impose upon you since mostly society is corrupt and such corruption can never bring happiness.

path you see to be true even if the entire world is against
ill find true happiness and the true meaning of your life
ch a path. Remember, society will generally tell you one
thing - do totally the opposite behind the curtains. Such way of
living can never make one happy.

-Stop seeking happiness in material possessions, as happiness can
never be found in things. Only pleasure can be found in things, but
happiness and pleasure are entirely different. Prepare your house,
open the window and the breeze will find its way.

-Learn to end everything psychologically at the end of each day to
make a fresh start the next morning. Do not continue to hold onto
your hurt, anger, jealousy, or even enjoyment, because only in ending
is there a new beginning to look at life with fresh eyes.

-Accept "what is" which is the current facts of your life. Never fight
with "what is." Just accept it with ease but do your best to change it,
if you like, but learn to be contented with what you have currently.
Be strongly aware that the most important thing you must have is a
healthy body. Do not let the "desire for more of anything" to be
deeply rooted within yourself because there is no end to such desire
and it prevents you from living joyfully with what you have now. If
more comes, naturally welcome it, but do not let this thing be the
master of your life.

-Always be aware to preserve the quality of love in your heart because
joy cannot touch a heart without love.

-Meditate upon this question sometimes; "Will happiness knock on
our door at a certain time as an invited guest while we are expecting
and getting prepared for it, or will it come totally unexpectedly
anytime?"

Letter#3
May 23rd. 2012

"Life takes place only in this present moment, whereas our minds live
either in the dead memories of the past or a projected future.
Therefore we never really live."

**Living in the present moment and moving with the natural
flow of life**

Living in the present moment is an art by itself that has the power to open the door to joyful living. One must understand how one's actions in daily life are time bounded. This means our minds meet the present moment either from the conditionings of the past memories or from the hope and expectations of a projected future. And therefore such a mind can never actually meet the present moment free from time to live and rejoice in it fully free from worries, fears, and anxieties which can only live in time but never can take root in the present moment itself.

When one begins the journey of self discovery in the search for one's "unique" secret key, one will naturally begin to realize that most of the time one does not live in the present moment but, rather, one lives in the river of time where all confusion takes its roots. And such realization itself brings a quality of attention and awareness which will then bring one more and more back into living in the present moment, which is the secret garden of the kingdom of happiness. And the irony is, most of us can not see this garden which is right in front of our eyes just because our minds got so stuck in time.

The absolute fact is that each and every single moment of our lives are taking place in this present moment which is called "The Now", but we can hardly experience life fully because our minds live mostly in thoughts which are rooted either in the dead past memories or a projected future. So there is a fundamental conflict going on in all our lives between the absolute fact of life, which in this present moment is the only time to live, and our minds living in time either of the past or the future. By such realization one begins to live more and more in the present moment, and this puts one on the natural flow of life and there comes a quality of "effortless living". The word "effortless" here implies "inner effortlessness" only and not the outer. One has to live in the world, and that implies effort in the physical world, but one can live an effortless life inwardly and that simply means elimination of all inner conflict. Like a good surfer moves with the flow effortlessly by becoming one with it, one will also begin to live this way of moving with the flow of life, and such wise way of living will bring one the best that life can offer. In this flow, right things and people will begin to come at the right time with perhaps

cidences and one's life will move very smooth towards
d happy destination.

Prac.... ιggestions on living in the present moment:
-Be aware of your lack of attention for what you are doing. You
might be walking, talking, eating or washing the dishes. Our minds
generally have a very strong tendency to wander away in time
thinking about something else while we are doing a certain thing.
Therefore the attention of the mind gets divided and we never really
do what we are doing with full attention.
-Do not label certain activities in your daily life as unimportant. For
example, you might not like waiting for the bus or spending time in
the toilet and you might see them as unimportant. But what is
ultimately more important is to stay in present moment fully all the
time, because only then we become one with life and be happy "only"
for being alive. So when you are waiting for the bus, wait for it by
staying in the moment with full attention to things around you
passing by.
-Once in a while do "living in the present" meditation. Just choose a
day or a few hours some time, and within that period of time live like
your past and future is totally removed. After this temporary period
ends you can come back to your normal life. But just for a little
period of time, live like there is no past or future but that moment
only. Once you start doing this meditation you will see more and
more you will begin to live totally in the present moment naturally at
other times as well, and you will love it because there is great joy of
living in it.
-End everything psychologically at the end of each day. Do not carry
your anger, hurt ... etc to the next day because their continuity
prevents you to live in the present moment fully
-Be aware of unnecessary thinking. Sometimes, for one thing, 5
minutes of thinking will be enough, but we think on such a thing for
hours or days, and such thinking will prevent us from living totally in
this present moment because we can't be totally attentive to the
"now" while we are lost in thinking.
-End attachments with ease without conflict. Attachment has its
roots in the past and therefore it blocks you to be fully in this present
moment.

-Imagine you were born on another planet like Mars, and that you came to earth for a holiday only for one week. How would you live on earth then? Would you not get mesmerized by the immense beauty of life itself only, and would you not enjoy the experience of life with its great beauty? Wouldn't it be like an ecstatic dream? Of course, after a week the problems of living we currently have would begin taking their roots again soon. If it is only a week, then we would live like a guest to enjoy it fully. The problems start only when we stick to it to be the owner of the house rather than staying as a guest just to enjoy. So, can we live on this earth as a guest ready to leave any time rather than taking deep roots? And the absolute fact is that we are nothing but just guests on this earth. It does not matter how long we live. As long as we want to take deep roots, there will be eternal conflict between the fact of being a guest and the desire to be the owner. So can we live on this earth as a guest all the time like that very first 1 week of arrival to earth for the first time? Not being attached to anything and therefore ready to leave any time as a guest would. Seeing the beauty of life anew with fresh eyes every morning, just like the first time of seeing life at that very first arrival to earth for a week of holiday. Meditate upon why we can't live our weeks like that very first week.

- As long as time has its effect on you, you cannot live fully in the present moment. Be aware of your changing moods on certain labeled days of the week such as Friday, Saturday or Monday...etc. In reality, there is no such labeling of any given day. Each day is simply a day. We need these labels in order to make plans and function, but see how our mood depends so much on these labels of days, and free yourself from them. As long as our mood is affected by such labeling, we will inevitably be enslaved by time, and therefore we will not be able to enter into the stillness of the present moment with its peace and joy. Just simply be aware of this kind of time effect on your mind, and this awareness will begin to free your mind from such time effect.

- Take each day of your life as a uniquely limited edition piece, and shape each one of your days like a skilled jeweler handcrafting a masterpiece with great love and attention, as each day will be the brick with which you will be building your eternal house. The beauty of your eternal house depends on the beauty of the pieces that make it.

you get on your car for a ride, if you are not in rush, just
ɔr about a minute after you get into your car. In this time
look at the things of your car attentively in silence. Just be
aware ʜe details you probably have never looked at closely before.
By doing this, in a subtle way you are opening a new dimension
which is out of the river of time because you have always been
starting your car soon after you get in it in order to get to a future
destination. Now, you are not in your car just to get to somewhere in
future, but you are in it to be aware that you are in a machine called a
car, in a planet called earth in the universe. It would be a miraculous
thing for an intelligent creature that has never been to earth to have
this experience of driving a car; whereas it has become an ordinary
affair for us because time makes us accustomed to it; therefore it
curtains the miracle of life which can be perceived only in this
present moment. So, stop the flow of time in this 1 minute break of
awareness, and then start your car and enjoy the drive. You are now
driving your car not to a destination in the future, but you are taking
a journey into the now. Your destination is not in the future, but in
the now. Be aware that each living moment in your ride is in the now.
So, your entire journey is in the now, and that means you moved
from present to present, and not from the past to a future
destination.
- Sometimes, when you are not in rush, get out of the river of time
which seems to be flowing from the past into the future, and go
deeper into the present instead. Think of your life as a movie for a
second; a 60, 70 or 80 years movie. What happens if somehow all the
film is burned, except a10 minute distance beginning from now.
Then, you would naturally go deeper into the present moment
because past and future is vanished. You would then do what you are
doing, whatever that thing is, with great attention because you do not
have a past anymore to cling to, or a future to project. It might be
washing the dishes, ironing, cooking, talking, singing etc. You would
be doing what you are doing joyfully because all the film is burned
except this 10 minute part. Therefore, there is no past or future to
dominate or shadow your relationship with the present. And, the
more you burn the film the more you enter into the depths of the
present moment. You can burn all the film except 1 week, or 1
minute, or 1 second and go deeper and deeper into the present
moment totally moving away from the river of time which flows

from the past into the future. The shorter the distance of the film left to live with, the deeper you go into the present moment, and basically there is no limit or end to the unknown depths into the present away from time, and joy of living will meet you there. Burn the film sometimes, and go deeper into the present moment.

- When you have some free time with no rush, try opening a door with full presence. Simply, go to a door in your house like the living room or bedroom door, and close the door. Now, first stand next to the door, and look at the door with full natural attention for some time. Look carefully at the qualities of the details of the door like the shape, color...etc. Do it like you have just awakened to life in the vast universe out of nowhere without a past or future, and the first thing you see is this door; similar like a baby looking at something for the first time. Of course it won't be easy, but just do your best. Then, slowly start opening the door like you are opening it for the first time, because as explained there is now only this door and you in the vast universe with no past and future. This implies that you will open the door with the care of full attention and presence in the 'now' like there is a little baby sleeping behind the door. Do this from time to time, and each time a new quality of attention will come. And this might sound strange, but in fact when you really can open the door with total attention in the 'now' totally free from the past and the future, then the quality of attention and the timeless presence in that very act of opening will be the door opening to the light of joyful living.

- Hold an item in your hand like a pen, bottle etc. and look at it silently. Be aware that you are making a subtle unconscious division between 'your hand' and 'the item' in the sense of hand being 'yours' as a part of 'your body'; and the item, not a part of your body. So, the eyes look and see 'your' hand, and the 'not your' item. So, the division is about 'yours', and 'not yours'. Can you look in such a way that this division disappears, and there is only 'the' hand holding 'the' item, so that there is unity between your hand and the item? If you try, you will see this will be possible only when there is looking without the 'ego' or the 'observer'; because as long as there is the ego looking there should be 'ego's' hand holding the 'not ego's' item. If you try you will also realize how difficult it is to end this division because the ego is so very deeply and strongly rooted in us. But, try this meditative exercise from time to time because it will bring a deeper awareness of the ego, and therefore a deeper awareness of living in the present moment because ego is rooted in time, and the very awareness of this is to be present in the 'now'. This is what is meant by the unity in the universe. When there is no ego, then there is unity simply because ego is the very factor of division. You will also feel a subtle sense of peace coming in while you are doing this exercise. It is also great fun. Enjoy!

Letter#4
June 9th. 2012

"Magic magnet of life will be given to those who become the master of living."

The law of attraction. Life & Wealth mastery

What is implied in the concept of "The Law of Attraction" has been in the interest of many throughout history, and only recently it has been given a certain name. It basically implies attracting things you desire to your life by using the law of attraction. This subject is quite a delicate one, and again, to apply law of attraction into one's life one must take the step to discover one's "unique" secret key first because no general formula can be applied to one particular human being without first discovering oneself through the search of the secret key. The very process of searching for one's "unique" secret key is the process of knowing and understanding oneself. And when one discovers one's secret key, then the law of attraction will find its right place with a special meaning.

Passion, desire and love are at the heart of the concept of the "Law of Attraction" but what is implied by passion, desire and love is very much different than their rather corrupted meanings in today's life. Our understanding of these words have become quite superficial currently, whereas at the greater depths of the inner journey of discovery, these things have much more valuable meanings with extraordinary energy which can be the center of attraction with great strength. Desire can become the burning flame of life if it finds its proper place.

To become the absolute master of one's life in the art of life mastery is one of the most important things to understand since we only live once, and this life is too precious to be wasted by living unconsciously like the dust in the wind being pulled in any direction. We must be very careful on this path by being the intelligent designer of our lives, because life is an eternal creation which can be built once only. We can not go back to our past and do some alteration in our lives. It is very important to understand that life itself is the greatest wealth and present we are given; much more important than its content, which is the material things of the world. But we generally get lost in the content, totally forgetting life itself which dwells beyond all that content. It is like an actor getting lost in a horror movie, totally forgetting the fact that he is simply performing in a movie. Of course life is not a movie but most of the time we forget we have our precious existence in this miracle of life because very often we get lost in the material content of it.

The more such awareness and love of life itself take root in us, the happier, healthier and more balanced we shall become. Currently, we are totally lost in the content and therefore very confused. The awareness of what is beyond the content will bring the light which shall dissolve this confusion. At the moment of **total awareness of being alive**, darkness of any kind shall disappear immediately. Once we understand this well, then we will have a totally different relationship with the content of life. Rather than getting totally lost in the pleasures of being attached to the content such as our cars, furniture, houses ... etc, we shall have a childlike joyful relationship with such content in which there is no attachment and therefore no fear of losing those things. Attachment, pleasure, pain and fear are inseparable by their nature, and such awareness of the miracle of life itself will have the ultimate effect to free the mind from the prison of this vicious circle. This awareness of **life itself** naturally goes together with the realization of how important a healthy body is. The real wise is the one who realizes the extreme importance of a healthy body for the full experience of the miracle of life.

So there must be a healthy balance between living with the things of the world which are the content, and keeping this strong awareness of what is beyond, which is **life itself**; so that we do not get lost in the content but see the whole picture all the time. And this very balance itself is the greatest form of wisdom in living which will make one the absolute master of one's life. Wisdom is always the simple way, and to put it simply, the very **love of life itself** is really the secret key of life. Together with this quality of life awareness, love of life itself will naturally take its strong roots in our minds and hearts. This implies loving life for itself per se and not for its contents, though contents have their right and necessary places. It is similar to loving our husbands or wives firstly for themselves rather than what they give us materially. And the stronger the quality of such love for life, the more apparent our **"unique"** secret keys become. So, loving life with greater and greater passion is the secret key to be discovered.

Wealth mastery is not a separate subject from becoming the master of one's life as explained above, and it is also very closely related with **The law of attraction** concept. Together with the art of Life Mastery and its immense wisdom, one will have the necessary tools to gather the wealth needed very easily. Then it will only be a question of what will be the right amount of such need that will differ from person to person. The answer to this question becomes quite closely related with the wisdom of the art of life mastery, and then the art becomes finding the right amount of such need.

An important tool to understand in wealth mastery is to see the fact of our outer lives merely as being a reflection of our inner, and this basically means life outside is simply a mirror reflection of our inner state of the mind. And to change the reflection on the mirror, the origin looking at the mirror must be changed first. So wealth creation first starts in our minds. There are many things involved in this, such as removing all mental limitations, which are created by the image making mechanism of our minds. For instance, as long as one has the image of oneself as the one who will always live in an apartment, one will most probably never own a house with a nice garden. Immediate destruction of such images "now" without allowing the poison of time is an absolute necessity. Since life takes place only at this "present moment", a new consciousness that is free from the limitations must be built in order to start the process of making one feel wealthy "now" and not in the future, because that kind of psychological future is a total illusion which will never come.

Another very important factor which greatly blocks the right workings of the law of attraction for our lives is psychological fear. One might somehow realize the fears on the surface, but the ones rooted at the deeper layers of our consciousness are not easy to realize and face. And, such fears which have taken deep roots must be seen, faced and removed for the law of attraction to work well in our lives. Unless this is done, our lives outside will merely be the mirror reflection of the inner; therefore such deeply rooted fears will create the dark mirror reflection in our daily lives. Fear is an extremely important subject to be delved into because unless the darkness of fear of any kind is totally removed from our consciousness, joy cannot get into our houses. Fear must first be realized and then be faced without any form of escapes. Fear can exist only if we refuse to face it. Fear is like the dark shadow chasing one all the time, and the moment one stops and looks at this thing very closely then it comes to an end.

Practical suggestions on the law of attraction:
-Be aware of any kind of limitations in your mind about your capabilities. Everything is possible in this world if you learn to live consciously by becoming the master of your life.
-Love life because love of life with great passion will create a very strong attraction for the things you desire.
-Feel yourself living the life you desire. Feel it "now". Do not think your desired life **will** come to you sometime in the future. If you do, then it will never come because in reality there is only this present moment. A projected future is an illusion. So you must feel it **is coming** to you now. Not that it **will** come to you, but it **is** coming to you **now**. If you think "it will", then that illusionary future will never come. So you must change "now" the state of your consciousness, and your life will start changing at that very moment.
-Once you change your consciousness this way, then feel 100% confident about the law of attraction's work in your life. Just like the food you ordered in a restaurant, things are on the way, coming to you now. You have no doubts about whether the food will come or not once you ordered it in a restaurant.
- The law of attraction is fundamentally about the quality of communication between you and the universe. Just like the radio

transmitter, the signals transmitted by you must be strong enough to be clearly received and heard by the universe. The strength and the quality of those signals depend on the quality of your inner psychological energy. If this energy at the source of transmission is strong, then the signals will be clear and strong. The quality of your inner energy depends on your inward clarity. If you eliminated inward conflict of qualities such as jealousy, hatred, fear, feeling of loneliness, attachment, anger... etc. then your inner energy becomes lucid. And, together with right meditation, love with its light of joy begins to radiate at the very origin of your inner energy field. This then brings about the highest form of energy which will transmit the strongest signals establishing a perfectly flawless connection between you and the universe for the law of attraction to have effect in your life with great precision. It is like getting connected to the central computer of life wirelessly to command certain changes in your life. The better the quality and coherence of the wireless signals sent out, the more the chances that they will be received by the central computer. The key, then, is the harmony of love and the light of joy in your inner spiritual life.

Letter#5
June 20th. 2012

"You will begin to live only when you enter into the silence of meditation."

True meditation in silence of the mind

This word meditation in today's world has more or less lost its meaning, since now it is generally understood as a set of formulas of breathing techniques or mantras to be repeated in the mornings, in order to attain quietness of the mind. Some even go further to seek so called "enlightenment" by mere repetition of certain words or mantras. As once mentioned by great philosopher Jiddu Krishnamurti, by such repetitions of mantras one might have many experiences of different kinds but it will never be the real attainment of this true quality of peace and quietness of the mind with its joyful effects in one's daily life. Meditation is not something separate from one's daily life to be practiced only 10 or 15 minutes in the mornings.

Sitting quietly for some time in the mornings will surely help us to start the day more relaxed, but this is only a small part of what is implied in meditation, and there is much more to be understood in the art of meditation.

Meditation must be there all through one's daily life, when one is talking to another, waiting for the bus or eating, and this is the beauty of meditation. No formulas, breathing techniques, repetition of certain words or mantras purchased at a certain price can bring this genuine quality of peace to the mind, but true mediation will naturally start taking place when one starts this inner journey of discovery. It will flower without one even realizing when one dives deep in to this river which is the inner journey of discovering oneself. Such meditation denies all forms of forced quietness brought about by any formulas, but rather it aims for the true silence which can exist only in the total freedom of the mind.

Practical suggestions on meditation:
Please bear in your mind that there is no static methods that can take you into the dynamic ocean of mediation; therefore be very careful not to make the below simple exercises into some static forms of methodical meditation; as doing so will destroy the vital quality of meditation. Do not get stuck in these exercises, but rather use them as a boat of understanding which must be destroyed when you cross the river and reach the other shore.
-Sit down quietly for 10 to 20 minutes in the mornings. Just do nothing inwardly and sit quietly without moving the body. Let all thought come out freely. Do not judge, stop or change them. Let them flower in such freedom, and you will see after some period of time they will begin to slow down naturally without forcing them to slow down.
-Question everything about what others say about living. Giving serious thought to your life this way is part of meditation.
-Try to be in the silence of nature as often as possible, and that silence naturally will bring a meditative quality to the mind.
- Spend some time looking at the mirror sometimes when you are not in rush. Just look at the mirror, and see your physical body. Then, look at your eyes in the mirror very attentively, and try to see the 'you, yourself, or ego" through your eyes in the mirror. Be aware that

both your physical body and your ego are reflected on the mirror. To see your ego on the mirror demands a silent and deep looking like that of a baby's. Just look in deep silence and you will begin to see this living 'you' on the mirror just like you see your physical body. If you do this mirror meditation sometimes, you will realize that after a period of time self awareness will be sharpened. This very ability to see your persona or self on the mirror is the ability to see the Aura. The more this ability is sharpened through such self awareness, the more clearly the Auras are perceived. When once this ability begins growing within you, then you will naturally get more and more acutely sensitive to perceive people's Auras instantly. This means you will see their true self behind the masks immediately without taking time, and this will naturally prevent you to waste your time with some people who have extremely subtle masks.

- Right now, after reading this, can you come into the presence of this moment for about 1 minute? Just simply get out of any rush you are in and relax; then stop all inward activity which is thinking as well as any outward activity you might be engaged in, and be silently aware of the physical space you are in. Just look quietly around, and be aware of the objects that fill the space. See their shapes, colors etc. Look attentively at any little detail which you never looked at before carefully. Be present and aware like this one minute period is the only time of your life. This means no past and no future. You will also feel a sense of time slowing down in this 1 minute period. Presence in the now slows down the river of time, and through the door of such slowing down of time, peace begins to come in. Do this sometimes to open the door more and more.

- Watch the thinker in your mind closely, and you will realize at that moment a higher level of consciousness will be activated. When there is such watchfulness of the thinker thought will slow down, and this very watching of the thinker will be the entrance door to the dimension of meditation. Then, you will begin to go into the deeper states of meditation when you begin also to watch the watcher. In this journey towards your inner depths with such flowering of meditation, there comes a moment when the division between the thinker or the watcher and the watched disappears; leaving the mind in an awakened state of bliss without a center, and therefore without a periphery. And, this state is the universal unity or the ultimate truth with its unshakable peace and joy.

- Take an analog clock or watch, and spare your 5 minutes sometime for clock meditation. Make sure you spare some time when you have no rush for anything. Simply watch the clock in these 5 minutes, and be aware of the time movement silently and passively. What is important is to be deeply aware of the river of time carrying us into the future. Just be aware silently. Be aware of the synchronized movement of the inward clock moving into the future while the outer is moving clockwise. This very silent awareness of the movement of time itself is the awakening of presence in the now. And, you will experience a sense of time slowing down in this silent awareness, and such presence will be the entrance door to a peaceful meditative state of the mind.

- What is the self, the thinker or the observer? Basically, what is this thing called 'me'? This question itself if pursued deeply and seriously will take one on the spiritual path of wisdom and realization. The moment this question is put seriously, a shaking awakening will begin taking place in the mind because this question will act as the alarm bell for the sleeper in the mind. With this question, the mind will begin being aware of the sleeper; therefore the sleep itself. This very awareness of the sleep itself will be the awakening process, and going deeper into this question will be the flowering of meditation towards greater inner depths.

Letter#6
July 10th. 2012

"True spirituality can be found in the only temple which is our heart. Love truly and you will be spiritual. That is all you need to do. In such spirituality, love becomes the religion; life the worshipped, celebration of each day dancing in ecstasy the ritual, and heart the only temple."

Spirituality & Self Discovery

Without self discovery, which comes through observation and understanding of oneself in relationships, there can not be a truly spiritual life. Such spirituality implies going beyond the pettiness of oneself to find out the ecstasy of life. And, in order to go far in the adventurous inner journey of going beyond oneself, one must start very near. And very near is beginning to know oneself.

The one who is really spiritual is the one who does not have an image of oneself as "The spiritual one". Such person will be the one who is living a life of freedom and its ecstasy. Such freedom and joy of living can not be separate from having a genuinely good heart full of love and compassion which is the very essence of a spiritual life. But all such qualities must flower naturally with the understanding that will come through self discovery rather than being artificially built by a book or a guru who will give certain directions for a so called spiritual life. In the true spiritual journey there is absolutely no place for the following of any kind of "authority"; as in this journey one is both the master and the disciple.

Such person who has mastered the art of joyful and creative living will naturally have a spiritual life without making any effort to be spiritual. In such spirituality, love becomes the religion; life the worshipped, celebration of each day dancing in ecstasy the ritual, and heart the only temple.

Practical suggestions on spirituality:
-Understand love is the essence of a spiritual life, and without love there is no spirituality, but do not try to find a particular way to love. There is no such a thing as how to love. Love must flower naturally like the love of a mother for her baby. Love can not be learned from books or others. And you can not go towards it because it has no laid down particular path to it. Just be aware of what love is not and such awareness itself will become the waves of love touching the shores of your heart. See love is not jealousy, hatred, selfishness or comparing ourselves with the others.
-Understand that love and selfishness can not go together, and just be aware of selfishness with all its subtlety in your relationships with others. Do not try to be unselfish in order to be good, spiritual or loving because trying to be unselfish in order to be good is still the activity of selfishness at a more subtle level. True goodness which has no selfishness in it must flower naturally because of seeing the danger of selfishness. Trying to build a good personality is just another game of selfishness. What is important is seeing and ending selfishness

completely in any direction rather than building up an unselfish personality which really has no meaning.

-Never accept the authority of another in the spiritual area. Listen to what others are saying because wisdom implies one must have a state of mind which says "I do not know"; therefore one is totally open minded, and only then one can truly learn. But, always find out for yourself the truth or the falseness of what is being said by the others.

-Be aware that love is the secret doctrine which by itself will easily bring perfect order, balance and happiness to our lives.

- If all those who believe in God would have humans as the object of their worship rather than some images of a dead god, then perhaps the living god could descend upon earth. God in the churches, mosques, temples or so called holy books is dead. Such worship of the dead images of god divides humans, and then they kill one another in the name of such god; never realizing the fact that killing another human being is killing the living god in the name of the dead one. Life that dwells in humanity is the true living temple to be worshipped, and in that temple humanity is one big family with no divisions brought by worshipping of the dead temples. Unless one has a taste of worshipping in this temple by getting lost in the ritual of that mad and true love for another human being, one can never know what truth or true feeling of being spiritual is.

-Meditate upon these questions; "Who is truly spiritual? The one who has practiced methods of meditation or silencing the mind all one's life or the one who truly loved even for a moment of one's life? Is love the factor of opening the spiritual eye or any kind of spiritual methods prescribed by the latest gurus at a certain price? Can there be a spiritual life without love at the very center?

Letter#7
July 30th. 2012

"The true artist is the one who has mastered the art of living."

A fresh approach to the art of creative living

The mother of all arts is the very art of living itself, and unless one understands such art totally and lives with it, life will have little meaning whereas life must have great depth and meaning rather than the superficial thing we have made it into. To understand and master such art of living one must have a totally fresh approach. One must leave behind all that has been said by others about how to live since each one must find his or her "unique" secret key to discover such art, and for this all formulas set by others must be denied in order to make a fresh start. Life is a dynamic thing which is ever changing, and no static formula of the past which is dead can be applied to such a living thing.

So in order to discover such art of living one must set aside all experts, gurus, and masters with all their formulas of how to live and how to be happy. Only then one will have a totally fresh approach to discover the truth of this matter for oneself by deep diving into the river of oneself for an adventurous inner journey of joyful discovery. If we go river diving we can observe and see things for ourselves without the help of an instructor next to us informing us all the time. The instructor's job can be giving certain information at the beginning, and then we will have to jump into the river and discover the great depths by ourselves, and this is the beauty of the art of creative living. After a certain point, one must not depend on anybody to dance with life in its ecstatic rhythm. The instructor will leave you once you learn to dance with your husband or wife by yourself, and the whole point of the art of living is that one must be able to perform it after some time without the help of the instructor.

This is about being a free spirit person to dance with life alone without the help of another. And, such freedom is in the nature of the universe. This free dance with life is a dangerous one in the sense of adventurous living.

Practical suggestions on creative living:
-Find out what you really love to do and you will naturally be creative there.
-Do not become a second hand human being by approaching life with certain static set of formulas given by others.
-See the fact that creativity can never come through the knowledge of books. Creativity must express that which is uniquely new and has never been seen before; therefore knowledge which has its roots in

the past memory can never bring about this quality of dynamic creativity in living.

-Do not accept the authority of so called experts who will tell you how to live. You can listen to them, but you must find out the truth or falseness of what they say for yourself because if you do not, then you might accept things which are totally wrong; therefore you might waste precious time of your life.

Letter#8
August 8th. 2012

"Life is an endless conflict without harmony between a peaceful mind and a healthy body."

Balance and harmony between a peaceful mind and a healthy body

Most of the conflict in human life seems to be originating from the lack of harmonious living between a peaceful mind and a healthy body. Peaceful mind and healthy body must exist together to make one whole for a happy life. Together with the beginning of true meditation, such peaceful mind and healthy body will naturally come into being in harmony because of the elimination of conflict in the mind. And then a great sense of creative life energy naturally will burst to express itself in one's daily life. The physical body must be treated with great care and attention in order to keep it healthy and sensitive, because joy can visit only such a body which is treated as a sacred temple.

Practical suggestions on harmony between a peaceful mind and a healthy body:
-Do natural yoga exercises such as hiking in nature and swimming.
-Keep the body light, fit and healthy.
-Try to have a vegetarian diet as much as possible. Avoid especially red meat whenever possible.
-Go deeply into the question of meditation.
-Make sure to preserve the quality of love in your heart as love is a very healing factor both for the mind and the body.

-Do not take vitamin pills unless there is an absolute medical necessity. It is most likely that the lack of physical energy you feel is caused by the psyche. If there is not enough peace in the mind with its vital life energy, then the physical body will feel the lack of physical energy. Human body is a very strong ultra-intelligent machine, and if you do not suffer from starvation like those in Africa, then the food you eat will have enough for the body to be strong. Just try eating a variety of different food instead of eating the same thing often. Even those who are poor and who can't have enough variety of food have strong bodies because that is the nature of the body. It can stay strong with little food. In most cases, the lack of physical energy we feel is not because we do not get enough vitamins, but it is because we do not have enough peace and happiness in the mind. Once the mind touches that true peace and happiness, then the body will have explosive physical energy. So, do not harm your livers with such pills. If you feel anything by using such pills, then it is most probably the placebo effect.

- Unless your weight is too low or you are suffering from problems of gaining weight, then make a mantra to yourself by saying **"I eat too much"** after each meal you have it does not matter how much you eat. Very often there is a truth to this both because we generally eat more than the body needs as human body is originally designed to survive with very little but right food, and also because we are aging by each passing day; therefore we must eat less and less. If you repeat this mantra of **"I eat too much"** after each meal by seeing the truth of it, then an awareness will grow, and you will see by time you will begin to eat less and less naturally without making any effort or conflict of diets . You must see the truth of it though for this to work as otherwise you will deceive yourself. Looking at and being aware of even a tiny little bit of fat particles in any part of your body will help you to see the truth of eating too much because our bodies must have zero amount of **excess** fat below the skin.

- Eat whenever you feel hungry just as much to feed your hunger, but make sure with a few minutes of silent observation that the hunger signals are coming from your stomach rather than your mind. There is nothing wrong to eat when the biological body wants it, but if you listen very carefully to the voice of the body you will see that the biological body needs little food whereas the mind needs much more. So, there is no need to control our eating with special diets.

Such controlling will only further the conflict of eating, but just become aware whether it is the body or the mind which is eating, and such awareness will make the best diet for us naturally and easily.
-Walk regularly, and live close to nature if possible.
-Try to stay away from stress at all costs.
-Do not keep things inside you, but rather express them openly. Never keep hatred in your heart. Jesus wisely said, "If you bring forth what is within you, what you bring forth will save you. If you do not bring forth what is within you, what you do not bring forth will destroy you."
-Avoid eating non-organic and Genetically Modified foods. Try to have a vegetarian diet as much as possible. If you have to eat meat, reduce the red meat amount to the very minimum, and occasionally ask yourself why you eat meat. Do not be overweight.
-Do not consume excessive amounts of alcohol. Prefer red wine if you drink.
-Do not smoke. Smoke less and very light if you have to. If you do, you must heal the body from the effects with an exercise in nature therapy.
-Do not forget that the best antidote for cancer virus is joy of love in your heart.

Letter#9
August 15th. 2012

"True confidence is the "natural" one only. Better to have no confidence rather than having an artificial one."

True confidence of absolute inner strength in business and personal life

In this journey of self discovery to find one's "unique" secret key, more and more a sense of true confidence, which will originate from the inner strength that one will naturally be gaining through the wisdom of self knowing, will show itself in one's daily life. Together with the gathering of physical and psychological energy, this natural confidence will act on one's personal and business life creating great positive difference.

Such quality of confidence is entirely different from the artificial confidence built by one's will and effort. This quality of natural confidence can come only through the journey of the search for one's secret key which brings wisdom and understanding in the river of self knowing. Since it is natural in this way, it will have extreme strength which will be felt immediately by anybody around because of the vibrant energy waves created. And such quality of strong confidence will naturally provide the mental energy needed for one to be the absolute master of one's business and personal life.

Practical suggestions on confidence:
-Be truthful in your daily life since truthfulness bears great quality of natural confidence within itself.
-Be what you are rather than trying to be somebody else other than what you really are. Be shy if that is yourself, and you will see if you are shy this way, then that shyness has its own confidence which is much stronger than the artificial, and therefore fake confidence.
-Tell your true opinion about things in a polite manner rather than telling things that you do not believe in just to please others.
-Practice aloneness as much as possible. Try to do things alone sometimes in order to be free from depending on others because true confidence can only come when one is able to stand on one's own feet psychologically.
-See the fact that when you really love others you become truly confident with no effort.

Letter#10
August 28th. 2012

"Discover the truth of life, and you will discover your purpose ."

Discovering your path and purpose in life

One must discover one's path in life, and the very discovery of this path in itself reveals the purpose of one's existence. Such discovery of one's true path is not separate from the search of one's "unique" secret key of life, and the very journey in this search itself sheds light upon our paths in life.

Practical suggestions on finding your path and purpose in life:
-Try to get out of the daily complications of your life. Look at your life from a distance without identification like it is somebody else's life. This way it will be easier for you to see the whole picture of your life and which direction your life is moving towards. When you begin to see the picture of your life as a whole this way, then the purpose will become more obvious naturally.
-See the fact that life is impermanent which means any purpose of the material type will be naturally very limited with little meaning. Therefore, look for a deeper and true purpose in life.

Letter#11
September 4th. 2012

"When the mind has its energy fully gathered, then stress can not take root."

Gathering and using of physical and psychological energy to its maximum to deal with stress

Gathering of life energy has extreme importance especially in today's busy and stressful life. Stress has now become one of the major causes of many serious diseases in life. Stress acts like a vampire to suck one's life energy, leaving one weak and vulnerable to such diseases to take root in the body easily. And, just like the vampire does not like light, so does stress; therefore it can not take roots and live when the light of joy has its strong existence in one's life. So, such light of joy is the only true cure to deal with stress since light and darkness can not exist together. There is no short cut or easy formula to this quality of real joy, but it will touch one in the very journey of self discovery to find one's "unique" secret key of life.

There are certain things one can do in order to prepare one's house such as having a right vegetarian diet as much as possible, keeping oneself away from environments and people which might help the dark thoughts take root in one's heart and mind, being in nature as much as possible ... etc. One must have a light and healthy body with a light feeling for this joy to find its way to one's heart. Opening the window for joy to enter is very closely related with opening one's heart to the perception of the natural beauty of the earth itself. A solitary walk in nature, watching the immense beauty of a sunrise or sunset and swimming are natural yoga activities which will prepare one's mind and heart for the flowering of the seed of joy. The body must have a strong and close relationship with Mother Nature and with her magic, subtle and secret touch.

Life will constantly throw upon us challenges, and if we respond to such challenges with our physical and psychological energy at its maximum, then such challenges will be very easy to deal with without having much of devastating psychological effects . Otherwise, such challenges can be very destructive for our lives in terms of our inner balance and happiness.

Practical suggestions on gathering your energy:
-Keep a light and vegetarian diet as much as possible.
-Always preserve a certain quality of relationship with nature as nature has a very subtle way of injecting life energy into our very being, and most of the time we do not even realize how such injection takes place because of the magical beauty of mother nature's secretly delicate way of dealing with us.
-Stay away from cigarettes.
-Do natural yoga exercises such as swimming and hiking in nature.
-Work more on "love" in the daily relationships of your life as love is the greatest energizer.
- If you feel your energy is being sucked by someone with bad intentions in a business meeting or elsewhere, just simply stay silent for a few seconds by focusing on a point in the room until you feel such sucking stops. This non-action of focusing on a single point quietly will act as a mirror which will reflect the vampire like energy waves coming from that person back to him or her. This way, you will preserve your energy and the other person will begin sucking his or her own energy instead of yours.
- Based on some scientific studies done, most of the animal species do not have a sense of self consciousness in the sense they cannot recognize themselves on the mirror. Of course, they have the physical senses which are part of the consciousness, but they do not have a sense of self awareness. This means they will never know death, and for them there is neither the past nor the future; therefore

only a timeless existence in the present. Different from animals, human brain which has the capability to function with an extraordinary level of intelligence do have a self consciousness. So, there is being conscious with the physical senses aware of the reality outside like that of the animals, and there is also the self consciousness which is the feeling of 'I'. Can the human mind go to the dormant room of being animal like conscious which means a body with fully awakened senses without a feeling of 'I', and then go to the room of self consciousness only when it is needed? Currently, human mind is in the room of self consciousness almost all the time centered around the 'I'. This creates conflict as a result because there is space of emptiness in the other timeless room which the mind needs desperately for energy. So, can the mind make this switch of going from one room to another whenever necessary so that it can live with more space and therefore with more energy and vitality?

Letter#12
September 11th. 2012

"Act **now** to live. If are you planning to act tomorrow, then you will be a dead living for the rest of your life."

Intelligent action from a clear mind

Action is a very important subject each human being should have a good understanding of. Our actions generally are not whole but rather broken up; to be regretted later on. A total action must be done fully in the present moment without having any roots in the past or a projected future. Such action then will be the right and intelligent action with no regrets. And when one begins to live one's daily life with such intelligent action all the time, then one will begin to live an intelligent life as a whole with no regret or pain of the wrong actions which have originated from ignorance of not knowing how to live rightly.

Also such action which is not conditioned by the past and therefore free from time, will become a part of the total movement of life which takes place neither in the past nor in the future but **now**. Action that is conditioned by the past can not have this total relationship with life because past and present are like two parallel lines which can never actually meet. So, such action in **the now** is extraordinarily important since living with right action in our daily lives will unite us with the natural flow of life simply because such action originates from the creative life energy itself. Therefore, without us even consciously realizing it, things in our lives will begin to move very smoothly. We all have particular times in our lives when things happen so easily and effortlessly and yet there are other times when everything goes wrong. This is all related with our state of mind and whether we are able to get into the natural flow of life in that particular time of our lives.

Therefore, this question of intelligent and right action becomes very important to understand since it is closely related with bringing absolute order into our lives as explained above. And, since such action will be totally connected to life itself at its very roots, it will move as one with life; bringing the best life can offer us often by strange and unexpected coincidences.

Practical suggestions on living with right action:
-End everything psychologically by the end of each day so that next morning will be the start of a fresh day of action free from the past.
-Do not make images in your mind about people or things because such images are time bounded, and they will prevent you to act totally in the present moment.
-When you begin acting in such a way, be well aware of the ego building a new image of itself as the one who is perfect in action. If this takes place then action comes to an end because this image which is actually the past will start meeting this present moment making the total action in the now impossible.

Letter#13
September 18th. 2012

"When you are simple inwardly you will be beautiful, because simple is beautiful."

Wisdom of simplicity

There is great wisdom in simplicity of living. Such simplicity is not much about living simple in our outer physical lives, but rather being simple inwardly which implies not complicating matters of life unnecessarily; especially through excessive thinking process. If we observe closely, we will see most of our thinking in our everyday life is unnecessary, but continuity of such repetitive thinking destroys the life energy within oneself. It is very important for one to understand the very mechanism of the machinery of thinking and give thinking its proper place to be used only when it is absolutely necessary. We need thought for certain things of our lives like finding our ways back home, but it seems thinking got out of the mechanical box, which is its proper place, by going into the psychological realm as 'the me'. And, it must be put back into that box again so that it finds its proper place of mechanical functioning only.

The wisdom that comes with such inner quality of simplicity will have great effect on the mind by slowing down the thinking mechanism which brings in fear, anxiety, feeling of loneliness ... etc. because when such quality of inner simplicity begins to take root in one's mind and heart then all complications of unnecessary thinking begin to vanish.

Practical suggestions on simple leaving:
-Be closely aware of the activities of your mind that wants more of everything. See the fact that there is no end to such direction of more and more. Such constant movement towards the more destroys the quality of inner simplicity. Wisdom begins with becoming happy with what one has. If more comes naturally that is ok, but building our lives totally based on this movement of the more will inevitably prevent us from appreciating life **at the present**. If we can't appreciate life **now** and be happy about it, then we can never be happy.
-See the fact that without an inner quality of simplicity love can not exist, and without love life has little meaning. So love, wisdom and inner simplicity go together.

Letter#14
September 25th. 2012

"Relationships are the mirrors in which we can discover and see ourselves as we actually are. And when you actually change by seeing yourself as you are in that mirror, then the world around you which is your mirror reflection will change as well."

Establishing right relationships and order in our lives

Relationship is one of the most important issues of life, and unless one establishes right relationships in life one's life is bound to be full of conflict. Relationship is the mirror in which we can see ourselves as we actually are . We can clearly see all our qualities such as jealousy, loneliness, anger, fear, attachment, pleasure, pain... etc. without any distortion in this mirror of relationship. Once we learn to look at this mirror of relationship in the right way then we can begin to establish right relationships in our lives. And, to be able to look at this mirror rightly is one of the greatest arts in life which demands great attention.

This art begins with seeing oneself in the mirror as one actually is without any distortion, and the very mastering of this art will itself establish right relationships with others. And, this art has great depths to be discovered, again, in the journey of searching one's "unique" secret key. In the process of establishing such relationship in our lives, the quality of the cosmic order will naturally start showing itself replacing the current confusion of our lives.

Establishing right relationships is also closely related with our understanding of **love** which is quite a corrupted word in today's world. Serious investigation into one's understanding of this word will bring about the truth beyond the word itself, and finding out the truth of **love** in our lives will have great healing effect on our relationships which are generally poisoned with **selfishness** which really is the total denial of the true meaning of love.

Practical suggestions on right relationship:
-Always be critically aware of yourself in your relationships. If everybody living on a particular street keeps in front of his or her

house clean all the time, then that street will always be clean easily and naturally. In the same way, if everybody in this world were critically aware of themselves then there would be no conflict on earth. Remember the fact that when you begin to change in such a radical way the world around you will also change as the outer world is merely a mirror reflection of the inner.

-Watch very carefully whether your actions in relationship have selfish motives of any subtle kind. Action of **love** is free from all selfish motives, and it is impossible to have right relationships without such action.

Letter#15
October 2nd. 2012

"Perfect order of the cosmos will come into your life once you become the master of time."

Time management

Being the master of time in life is one of the greatest arts that will bring one's life perfect order. Once this art is learned well, then one will use time very efficiently, and this will make great positive changes in one's personal and business life. The secret key of this art is hidden in the quality of relationship we have with time. Quite often time becomes our master instead of us being the master of time, and this can be changed by looking at time differently.

Can we use time simply as a measurement device just like measuring a physical distance? If we can, then we will never be in rush for anything. Why are we generally in rush to catch the bus or the train that we take every day? Just with a simple shift in our minds, we can change this totally, and this simple change will remove a lot of unnecessary pressure and stress from our minds.

If we observe carefully we will see that beginning a day in rush of any kind will not be the best start, and generally the day continues the way it starts. Also, if you have noticed, good things and coincidences generally take place in life when one is totally relaxed with no sense of rush because only then one can enter into the natural flow of life which will take us to our desired destination free from the confusion that arises with the pressure of time.

So why don't we make a simple change in our lives to take a step to use time as a simple measurement device so that we will not be in rush again. It is very simple. For example, if my bus to work is at 9 a.m. and the **time distance** between my home and the bus station is 15 minutes, then I have to leave home around 8:40 a.m. to make sure I will not be in rush. And let's say if my average time to get ready after waking up is around one hour, then to make sure there is no sense of rush, I should wake up at 7:30 a.m. Though it seems so simple, unfortunately most of the time we are in rush. If we can make this small and easy change in our lives, it will have great positive effects in return because the sense of being in rush is very destructive for the creative life energy simply because one can not live in the present moment when one is in rush. And, being well rooted at the present moment is the only way of deriving the vital life energy. When a tree is cut down, it dies because it is not connected anymore to the ground soil which nurtures her body. In the same way, when our connection with the present moment is broken then we wither away.

Therefore, learning to use time as a simple measurement device to plan our day has extreme importance. To remove this pressure of **rush** from our daily life means that our lives, from that day on, will be lived without this sense of rush, and this will also slow down time as time is relative. We must all have noticed that sometimes time passes quickly and some other times it slows down. Time will slow down when there is this sense of **no rush**, and life will have much more meaning then. Such an easy shift will change our lives forever because a life lived in rush is a totally different one than the one lived free from all the pressure and stress of rush. Just apply this simple thing to your lives and you will see how your life will change all of a sudden.

Time management has many different aspects as well. One of them is to plan our time well enough so that we can have enough time to give full attention to everything we need to do. The quality of such full attention for anything we do in business or personal life has immense importance because without such attention we can not do things properly and creatively. So, time management becomes extremely important for this reason as well. How shall we then have enough time for everything we do, and also have enough time to relax at the same time because we must have some time for our own just to relax? Without such relaxation, our minds can not have the emptiness needed for the creative life energy to be gathered to act in our lives to change things in a positive way. As a practical way, looking at time like a ruler to measure distance can help a lot for easy and proper time management. Basically, can we look at a day of 24 hours as a distance to be covered? Then, can we simply place things on this 24 hours distance like a meeting at 4 p.m. and a dinner at 7 p.m. ... etc? This demands that we look at this 24 hours from a silent timeless ground to plan it first, but if we are lost in the movement of time then we can never master time this way. When we are in the river of time and rush then the river becomes the master, but when we step out of the river then we can master the river. When one is in a naturally relaxed state of mind enjoying life then at such moments the mind is out of the confusion which is created when one is lost in time. This way of time management can be extended from a single day to weeks and years so that we can have intelligent and orderly lives. This can be done much more efficiently when the mind is quiet, therefore quietness of meditation becomes very important at this point. Together with such true meditation, our minds and the machinery of thinking will slow down, and this will bring about a great clarity of the mind. Such clarity with its particular quality of space and silence will help us a lot to be the masters of time.

Practical suggestions on time management:
-Plan your day at times when your mind is relaxed and clear.
-Use time as a simple measurement device to plan your day with efficient precision.

Letter#16
October 9th. 2012

"There is no business life separate from the personal one. Life is one unitary movement without such divisions."

Business life
Business is a part of our lives and doing well in business life greatly depends on our state of mind in general. Therefore, one must approach life as a whole. One will be very effective in business life if one is full of creative life energy. Such creative life energy will have great positive effects on one's relationships and communication in business life, and this by itself is the most important key one needs to open the door to one's desired achievements.

Life is relationship. Therefore the quality of relationships one will have with others in business is extremely important. In order to have such positive quality of communication in relationships, one must not separate life as the business and personal, because in reality they are inseparable. If one is unhappy and confused in one's personal life, then that will inevitably affect one's business life very negatively because one can not have creative life energy fully unless one has peace and balance in one's life. And, without such creative energy one's potential will be very limited in business life. If one looks at the lives of those who have reached the top levels in their area, one will see that one major common factor with all of those people is the fact that they all knew how to keep their creative life energy at its maximum most of the time. Conflict sucks that energy, therefore one must learn how to live a life with a certain quality of inner balance, harmony and peace which will make the mind very sharp and clear. Then, out of such clarity, one will act perfectly with natural intelligence in business life and such action will bring one's desired achievements in business life.

Practical suggestions on business life:
-See the fact that having the harmony of mental peace has great positive effects on business life.
-Do not compare yourself with others in business. Such comparison destroys the quality of creative energy which is extremely important for your business. You do not need to compare yourself with others in order to be good in your business. That is an illusory conditioning of the society today which, in fact, acts as a preventing factor rather than a supporting one businesswise.
-Find out what you love in business life. When you do business in an area that you really love then things will happen naturally with ease,

and happily. If you are in an area which you do not really love, then try to do that thing the way it makes you happy until you begin doing what you really love for a living.

-Celebrate good results in your business all the time.

-Be very understanding and generous to the people working for you. When you really love the people working for you, then there will be no need to force them to do things since they will be doing it willingly. Such love has a quality of energy within itself which will change things to the positive very easily and efficiently.

Letter#17
October 27th. 2012

"Without love life has very little meaning."

Love

It seems there are many different definitions of love in today's world. The love of one's country, the love of one's husband or wife, the love of one's house, car...etc. All such types of love are products of self-centered activity because there is always the "me" or the "ego" at the very center of such types of love. Can there be love where there is selfishness of any kind? Does not the very concept of "mine" imply selfishness of some kind? If this is so, then can there be a quality of love in which there is no sense of "me or mine"?

Can love exist where there is a division of the "me" and "her"? Or, love will exist only when such division of the "I" and "not I" comes to end totally? If one observes closely one will realize that our minds look at life always from such a divisive point of view. For us, life is defined basically as the "me" and "not me". For instance, when we look at a tree that tree is the "not me" and the "me" is looking at the tree. Similarly, we look at everything in life through such a divisive process. Can love exist in such division or love can come into being only when this division comes to an end? And, what would it mean then to look at a tree without such division? We all occasionally experience such perception in which there is no division as the "me" and "not me". For instance, when one sees the majesty and beauty of a great mountain for the first time, all of a sudden the magnitude of this immense beauty destroys the "me" for a split of second and then there is 'looking' without the division of the "me"; **just looking** at the beauty of that mountain. For a split of a second or two we experience this state of mind in which there is no division originated by the thinking process, and we truly enjoy that moment because that very moment in which the "me" disappeared is the moment of the mind entering the serene waters of the ocean of love where there is true peace, happiness and joy of life which is an entirely different thing from pleasure. Soon after having this marvelous experience for a second or two, the "me" with its chattering comes back again by saying; "How beautiful it was! I should come here and experience it again". But, this very moment of the "me" entering the mind again is the very moment of "love" leaving the heart simply because this state of "love" cannot exist together with the "me".

This happens in our daily life in many different occasions. For instance, we see a nice house with some marvelous ocean view, and the very first seeing of such a wonderful view puts our hearts in this state of love and happiness for a short time; then we decide to buy the house thinking we will find the happiness we have been looking for such a long time in this house. But, what generally happens after living in that house for a couple of months is that we do not even see that ocean view anymore, or even if we do it does not have the same meaning of that very first looking without the division as the "me or looker" looking at that view which is the 'looked'.

So the process of our minds is very simple. It experiences true joy of living in occasional moments where such division comes to an end, and then it makes it into pleasure when it begins to seek that very joy of the original moment. That very seeking is the activity of the "me" or the "ego" in its desire to experience the beauty of that original moment again, but the problem is that very seeking becomes the very cause of the existence of the "me"; therefore nonexistence of that other state which might be called as "love".

So the question then is, 'Can the mind live the joyful moment without division, and then die to it immediately without making it into a pleasure by seeking in order to experience it again'? That very seeking is the self-centered activity of the mind which denies and blocks love coming into being. That state of love implies seeing life anew with fresh eyes all the time, but if the mind says "I want to go there to that marvelous mountain and have that joyful moment again", then next time one goes there again, one will meet the mountain with the dead memories of the past whereas in the very first original seeing there was direct timeless perception with no memory; therefore past did not enter into the very act of "looking" at the mountain at that moment which was the present moment then. These memories of yesterday then become the "me" looking at the mountain and seeking the original joy of yesterday. This process creates the division of the "me" and the "mountain". So, we can never look at that mountain and life fully in this present moment with fresh eyes in that state of love because of this pleasure seeking process of the mind which is time bounded.

For that state of love to come into being, all self-centered activity in any direction must come to an end totally. That state of love can never be "ours". It is like the wind outside. We cannot hold the wind in our hands. Similarly, love cannot enter into the prison of the "me" since love is free. The very desire of the mind to capture again that original moment of the experiencing of joy without division is in fact the impossible attempt to hold on to that thing which cannot be possessed. That state of love can never be invited or possessed by the "me" simply because it is totally and unconditionally free. And, that is the beauty of it.

When there is that state which might be called "love", then there is spontaneity of living. And, the action of love then brings richness of life. So, love is like the breeze outside which will come in as it will when the windows are open. The only thing we can do is to prepare our houses and open the windows which means ending all self-centered activities of the "me". This demands close attention, observation and watchfulness of the activities of the mind choicelessly in any direction. In this very process of observation and watchfulness love might come in unexpectedly, and it comes only when the 'me' which is that expectation is totally absent.

Practical suggestions on love:

-Be aware of your selfish motives in your daily life of relationship. Such motives can be open and easy to be seen or they can be very subtle and well hidden behind the curtains. So, close attention and awareness is needed. Just see such motives as they are without trying to change them, because the very desire to change them is again the movement of the limited self-centered activity of the mind in just a different direction. It tries to change them in order to have that so called state of love and joy. If you have any motives, conditions or expectations in return then love cannot exist because love is unconditional.

-Be alone sometimes especially in nature. Take a nice walk in the silence of nature as much as possible.

-Keep the body healthy, light and fit. Having a right diet is of great importance for the preparation of the house which is our body so that the breeze of love outside can pay a visit. A simple vegetarian diet as much as possible is strongly suggested.

- Can there be spirituality without true natural goodness in one's heart? The attempt to be good because the religions, the gurus or the so called sacred books said so is clearly not the goodness that flowers naturally. It is rather an imposed sense of goodness with very little meaning. Or, can any religious or spiritual ritual open the door to such flowering of love in one's heart? Obviously not; simply because dynamically living quality of love can not be born out of any mechanical repetitive practices. Love must be free from the time bounded cause and effect chain. There are now the new age spiritual movements of many different kinds all around the world where people talk about love endlessly. Goodness can come about only with this flowering of love in the temple of one's heart. When you actually love your friend, your children, animals or the trees; there is neither any cause in that love nor any rituals or the dead words of the so called spiritual books. There simply is causeless love bubbling in your heart. No books including the so called sacred ones, no practices, no beliefs or no words of love can open the door to that mysterious goodness of love.

- Instead of seeking love, be aware and try moving away from what love is not. Move away from environments and people in your life who lack love. Also, move away from what love is not within you; and that is moving away from jealousy, hatred, inward comparison etc. Try it, because this very movement away from what love is not might be the only way to love. Instead, we generally want to look for, seek or walk towards love. But, how can we walk towards the unknown which is timeless and anew each moment? We can only walk towards a known destination which means that thing must have its roots in the past, but does love have its roots in time or is love timeless? When we walk towards love, it is the idea of love we have in our time bounded minds that we are walking to. So, this very movement away from what love is not; rather than moving towards love might be the only movement that will take us to the vast ocean of love.

- To be able to live a day like it is one's last day, one must be able to leave the attachment to things with one timeless strike in the present moment just like death. Hopefully we will have long lives, but if death comes today are we well prepared to leave the world? Did we treat our loved ones and friends the way we would if today was our last meeting with them? What would be the quality of the expression in our eyes if those eyes knew they were looking at this beautiful world and human beings for the last time? Can we live this way in our daily lives? If we can't, then what is preventing us?

Letter#18
November 6, 2012

Wisdom and Happiness quiz
Please answer these questions very honestly without deceiving yourself because if you escape from unhappiness by deception then it will run after you like a dark shadow all your life. So, please take your time to think carefully before you answer in order to get a true and helpful result because the first step towards happiness is to be fully aware of unhappiness.

1-Can you sleep very well?
2-Do you really love what you do for a living?
3-Are you very fit physically?
4-Can you be happy without a cause and without depending on an object of any kind like your car, boyfriend, money etc.?
5- Do you have an adventurous spirit who likes living dangerously?
6- Do you often do things in which you feel very creative?

7-Do you enjoy being alone sometimes doing nothing silently without people around you? Have you been silently alone this way anytime in this past week?

8-Are you aware of the beauty of the nature like a sunset, the stars, the moon...etc. at least once a day for a minimum duration of 10 seconds each time you are aware? Have you been aware this way today for instance?

9-Can you be happy with your life as it is in this present moment without thinking of a past or future happiness? Are you happy right now just because you are alive?

10-Can you very easily stay for a month without any alcohol, smoking, legal or illegal drugs? Have you had a month like this in this past one year?

11-Can you easily sit quietly doing nothing for at least 10 minutes without being occupied with anything whatsoever? Have you had such 10 minutes in this past one week?

12-Does nature actually have a very important place in your life?

13-Are you a very simple person inwardly and also outwardly without desiring too much of luxury?

14-Can you simply enjoy things of life without being attached to them?

15-Are you seriously interested in finding a true and deeper meaning of life?

16-Are you free from authority in your inner life so that you are the teacher and the student on the path towards happiness?

17- Do you care for your health perfectly?

18-If you have to swim to a secluded island from a sinking ship, could you be peacefully able to accept the fact that you might have to live there alone for the rest of your life never being able to see your loved ones again?

19- Can you live with only proper food, clothes and shelter for a year and be happy just because of being alive, or you need more to be happy?

20-Are you ready and prepared to peacefully welcome death to your house anytime even if you hear your door is being knocked on now?

Please count the total number of "YES" answers you have given, and see your happiness and wisdom state from below scale.

0-3   YES   Very unhappy

4-7	YES	Unhappy
8-11	YES	Will survive
12-15	YES	Happy
16-18	YES	Very happy and wise
19	YES	Ecstatically happy and supremely wise
20	YES	The "enlightened" one

Letter#19
November 11, 2012

Life is the ultimate teacher

The philosophy of the Temple of Illumination which really is the school of life itself should be; "Life is the ultimate teacher". The teachers of this school must not depend only on the technical knowledge certified by a particular school because unlike other areas the school of life is about living itself; therefore no static technical knowledge however well certified can ever deal with the dynamic challenges of life totally. After all, no certification can give one the secret key to true happiness. And, how can one be a cure to another if one is suffering from the same disease? Happiness is a dynamically living "state of being"; therefore it can not be found by static means of any certified formulas. That means, one must go further to take an inner journey of discovery in to the great depths of life to find out for oneself the right way of living in great happiness. Such journey implies deep thinking, exploration and questioning of everything to find out the truth of life.

A "Fitness teacher" must be certified with the technical knowledge about fitness, and similarly in all other areas it is important for any teacher to be certified with the technical knowledge of that particular area. A "Life Coach" for instance should perhaps be certified as well, but life is too vast to fit into the knowledge of any technical certifications, and this vastness can only be discovered by this adventurous inner journey of discovery in which the ultimate true teacher who will certify its coach will be life itself.

True knowledge of life implies great passion to understand the truth of life. This demands constant observation, attention, awareness and questioning to find out. The meaning of the word "philosophy" in Greek is "love of wisdom" which can only come about by understanding life at great depths. So, the teachers of the school of life must have this quality of great love and passion to know life, and knowing life first starts with knowing ourselves. One must go beyond the pettiness of oneself in order to know the vastness of life, and one can go beyond only by self knowledge. Therefore the teacher must be a philosopher in the truest sense of that word which means he or she must go deep river diving into the school of life to find out for oneself rather than quoting from others since life won't fit into any quotation from the dead past as it is a dynamic process which is always new in the present moment to be met directly with fresh eyes and mind. And, that is the beauty of it.

To be a student and to learn from the silence of Mother Nature when one goes for a hike would be much more interesting, and it would teach much more about life than sitting in the small room of a school in order to learn life from books. The limitless quality of life can never be contained in the limited pages of any book.

Letter#20
November 14, 2012

"Philosopher is not the one who is lost in complicated thought. Philosopher is the one who is deeply passionate about finding the truth of life, and such truth can be found only with a quality of inner simplicity rather than complication of thought. The very passion to find the truth of life itself will build and shape the philosopher within naturally, and every human being who has such passion is a philosopher."

The Philosopher and Truth

The word "philosopher" has lost its true meaning in today's world just like the word "love" has lost its. The word "philosophy" comes from the Greek φιλοσοφία (philosophia), which literally means "love of wisdom". What is implied here by the word "wisdom" is related with searching the truth of life, but in today's world the first image of a so called philosopher is basically the one who has a thought mechanism which is much more complicated than the ordinary. So, there is a fundamental difference between the original meaning of the word which implies love of wisdom, and today's meaning which implies complicated thinking. Wisdom has nothing to do with complicated thinking, but it is rather the contrary which is inner simplicity and clarity of seeing. So, here, the word "philosopher" is being used in its original meaning; and by this definition, whoever is seriously interested in finding a deeper and true meaning of life is a philosopher simply because such person has this quality of love and passion to find the truth of life. One certainly does not need to know the history of philosophy or the complicated words of many different so called philosophers. One may read them or not, but what is most important is one must be an absolute light unto oneself, and never walk on this path with the light of another.

Such person must deny all so called spiritual authority of the others, whoever that person maybe, in order to find the truth for oneself because authority of any kind in the search for truth will inevitably prevent one from finding the truth. One can listen to what the others say, but accepting the authority of another destroys the most essential thing in this search which is doubt and questioning of everything. So, one will listen, and one will find out the truth or falseness of what is being said without accepting any sense of authority which brings nothing but dark shadows to this inner search. That means being a light unto oneself has extreme importance in this journey. Then, one will begin questioning the simple daily matters of life with this light, and walk from there to greater depths moving from one fact to another so that one will not get stuck in illusions by not leaving the solid ground of the facts . This very beginning in fact becomes the very end then, and there is no such a thing as an advanced philosopher or a beginner because wisdom is not something which is built through time. Wisdom, that clarity of seeing, can come to anybody at anytime. One does not even need to read any books. Sometimes, a truly happy and friendly smile on the face of a poor villager who never read the latest books might imply greater wisdom than that of the stressed and unhappy faces of those who read hundreds of books. Wisdom has nothing to do with knowledge which is gained through time. Wisdom can only come through timeless seeing. One can read thousands of books, and record the information as knowledge; but this does not make one wise. Computers can store millions of pages of information perfectly, but computers are not wise. They are programmed, and wisdom is also related with freeing the mind from all programs which are our human conditionings. That means knowledge can also dangerously condition the mind if one is not aware, and this might be a major factor of blocking the flowering of wisdom.

So, wisdom cannot be found through knowledge. One must rather be a student of life and learn through observation in relationship with things and people. One must learn to read the book of life to be such a philosopher and then love, wisdom and philosophy becomes inseparable in this joyful journey of the philosopher who is nothing but merely a simple student of life.

Practical Suggestions on being a philosopher:
-Do not accept the authority of another in your inner life. Find out the truth of things by being a light unto yourself.
-Learn to read the book of life by observation rather than getting lost in many books. And be the student of life rather than being the student of another whomever that person maybe.
- The word "philosophy" comes from the Greek φιλοσοφία (philosophia), which literally means "love of wisdom". 'Sophia' means wisdom in Greek, and philosophy which is love of wisdom can also be called as **'Love of Sophia'**. So, make sure you have your own love story with Sophia rather than repeating the love story of others. There really is not much point of talking about the love of Romeo for Juliet unless one knows that love first hand. In the same way, the love that Socrates, Aristotle, Jesus or Buddha etc. might have had for Sophia was the living fire then, but talking about their love of Sophia using the dead words have little meaning unless one ignites the original fire of love for wisdom in one's own heart. This is what is meant by **'Becoming a Buddha yourself'** in Buddhist teachings.

Letter#21
November 16, 2012

"There are two paths in living. Living factually or living in illusions. There is no third one. Living factually is the path of light whereas living in illusions is the path of darkness. Why not simply take the path of light?"

Living Factually

Living factually is one of the greatest arts in the life of wisdom. This simply means one must see the facts of one's life as they actually are, and then move from one fact to another. If one takes the journey of life this way then one will never get caught in the darkness of illusions.

First of all, are we capable of meeting the facts of our lives as they actually are? For instance, we might be in a relationship and the fact might be that our boyfriend or girlfriend does not really love but just takes the advantage of the other in many different ways. In such a case, a man or a woman who has mastered the art of living factually will take immediate action even if it may be painful momentarily, rather than deceiving oneself by thinking he or she loves; which means an escape from the fact; therefore living in the illusion of being loved by the other. So one can either live with facts or live with illusions. The two cannot coexist. And, as seen in this example, living factually implies intelligence whereas living with illusion implies lack of intelligence, because the factually living one will not waste his or her time with somebody who is taking the advantage of the other. She or he will take the immediate action which might be painful at that moment, but such action will prevent the disease of the relationship spreading more; thus causing much more pain.

Apart from this, one might have certain hardships in one's life from time to time. The one who is living with facts will pass through such hardships without many scars as the wisdom of accepting things as they are will take one to the safe shores through the stormy night. Accepting things as they are does not necessarily mean one accepts the current situation without doing anything to change it. It means acceptance of the situation today so that one does not suffer, but at the same time, one will do whatever one can to change the current situation for the better. So, what is most important is to pass through this challenging period of our life without inner suffering. We cannot freeze the time anyway; therefore we will have to pass through these challenging times. As there is no escape from it, the question then is; 'Shall we pass through this tunnel with or without suffering? Will it be a dark tunnel or a tunnel with at least enough light to see the path clearly? Wouldn't it be much wiser if could pass through the inevitable times of challenges without suffering if possible'? If we can totally accept the current facts inwardly, then there will be no suffering. The very origin and the cause of our suffering is this constant battle between the outer facts of our lives and the inner rejection to accept such facts. The wise is the one who accepts the facts of today as they are and who, at the same time, does his best to change these facts or conditions for the better; therefore he or she does not suffer in this period of transition. And, because there is no suffering one's mind will be clear and not confused. This clarity is what is most needed in dark times of our lives. In darkness, what is needed is light, and that means clarity of the mind. Otherwise things will get worse like that of a vicious circle.

Let's give a simple example to make it a bit clearer. For instance, if I lose my job today that will be a great shock to my life. What are my options? Either I accept this terrible fact inwardly so I feel peaceful and start looking for a job tomorrow, or I cannot accept this new fact of my life thinking it was a very well paid job with a good future career etc. and I lose my inner balance. These are the two options. If I take the first option by accepting this fact inwardly, then I will be healthy psychologically, therefore my chances to find another job easily will be much higher because when one's inward energy is heightened things happen much easier in life. If I take the second option by not accepting this fact then I will be destroyed psychologically, and my chances of finding a new job will be much lower. So, wisdom says take the first option simply because what is the point of taking the second one? Of course this is easier said than done, but if one sees what is implied one will naturally choose the simple and wise way which is to accept and live with the facts of our lives. As we have seen in this example, the wisdom of living factually becomes the light which will enlighten one's path in challenging times. Without such wisdom with its light, things will most probably get worse and worse.

Let's take another example which could be a much more difficult fact of life to be accepted. As a worst case scenario, one might be diagnosed with a serious disease like cancer. Again one has two options. Either an inner acceptance of this situation; therefore having peace of the mind or simply go crazy. This is also easier said than done, but if one can accept it inwardly then one will be peaceful and that light of peace might even cure the disease. The other is total confusion which will make things much worse. So, there are two paths to be taken again. In such a situation, the truth might be that one might live for another couple of months or so, but even then why not live the last period of one's life in the light of peace rather than in the terrible darkness of inner confusion. Wisdom is this inner simplicity of seeing that there are only two paths and because of this clear seeing one naturally takes the path of light. As mentioned above, these things are easier said than done, but possible only by great inner work of understanding oneself very deeply. Through the light of this understanding wisdom will naturally come and act in one's life and such way of living is the truly spiritual one. Spirituality is not in the temples or in the words of latest gurus, but it is in this light of wisdom which will come through self-knowing.

The Buddha was once asked about what enlightenment was, and he replied by simply saying; "The ending of suffering". The more one begins to accept and live with the facts of one's life as explained above, the less one will suffer; therefore get more and more enlightened. The ultimate form of enlightenment in this context is the total freedom from all inward suffering as the Buddha has very wisely pointed out so that one does not suffer at all inwardly. After all, we will live this life until the very end whether we like it or not; so why not live it without suffering instead of with it?

So, one has two paths of living this life. Living with the facts or living with illusions. As explained above, living with the facts will bring more and more light to our lives whereas living with illusions will bring more darkness. So why not simply take the first path and live with the facts instead of escaping from the facts; simply because it is much easier, wiser and happier this way.

Practical suggestions on living factually:

-See the fact that not accepting the facts of your life inwardly is a much more difficult path to take than accepting and living with the facts of your life.

-Accept the facts of your life inwardly and free yourself from inner suffering; therefore from confusion as well. Then, you will naturally have the clarity of the mind to take the necessary actions rightly in order to make the changes you desire in your life.

Letter#22
November 17, 2012

"A mind that is everlastingly seeking pleasure will move far away from the breeze of joy."

Is joy or true happiness related to pleasure?
What is pleasure? It is simply an experience which the mind likes and demands the repetition of. Such pleasure can be sexual, sensual or psychological as well. The desire to eat a certain food very often can be an example of a sensual pleasure whereas the desire to have power to dominate others will be a psychological one.

What is implied in all these forms of pleasures? First of all, pleasure must be self-centered. That means, in pleasure there will be an "I" or "ego" at the very center demanding such pleasure, and then enjoying the experience. The "I" will desire a certain type of beef for instance and then the "I" will enjoy the taste of it. Secondly, pleasure must be time bounded. It must have its roots in the past. For example, I have a certain experience today which I like, and I demand the repetition of it. So, first I must have an experience which I like, then the mind labels it as pleasure which is merely the memory recorded in the brain; therefore rooted in the past. There must also be an "experiencer" as the "I" who is experiencing together with an object of pleasure like some beef, good drinks etc. There is also always the "more" concept involved in pleasure principle. The "I" always wants more of a certain pleasure with greater intensity, or it wants new kinds of pleasures simply because same type of pleasure gets boring after some time like any repetitive thing.

And, what is joy? Joy is certain moments of life in which one feels happy unexpectedly without any planning. This joy might come to one when one is taking a solitary walk, when one is cooking, looking at a face or seeing a cute cat walking down the street...etc. It is not something that can be described clearly like pleasure by using words, but surely all of us must have experienced such moments of joy.

What is involved in joy? Firstly, it is not self-centered like pleasure because it is not something planned like pleasure. For instance, the "I" plans to have its favorite beef for tonight, then the "I" has the pleasure of it. So there is the "I" involved at the center in pleasure mechanism from the planning stage until the actual moment of experiencing that pleasure. But, in joy there is no such "I" who plans the moment of joy; therefore at the very moment of joy the "I" is not there as the "experiencer". The "I" comes back only a few minutes after the joyful moment saying, "I felt so happy". And, there is no causation in joy because it is not a repetitive movement like pleasure. In a repetitive movement, there is a cause of pleasure like eating one's favorite food. Joy can come anytime and anywhere without any particular reason, and because it is not repetitive like pleasure, it is free from time. There is no " the more" principal in joy as there is no "I" involved at the center. You don't say "I want more" of the real enjoyment of a beautiful sunset or the enjoyment of seeing a lovely and friendly face.

So, as explained above, joy and pleasure are fundamentally different things. And, if one has strong tendencies to seek pleasure, then this joy will be visiting very rarely because when the mind is in the state of seeking pleasure then the windows are firmly shut for the breeze of joy to find its way in. This does necessarily mean one should not enjoy things of life like a delicious food though. The question is; 'Can one enjoy things of life without turning them into pleasure"? This means; 'can one die totally to the pleasures once they are had without seeking the further repetition of them'? This does not mean one will never have that certain delicious food again, but can one just simply be aware of the activities of the "I" who turns the enjoyment of things into the repetitive movement of pleasure? And, if there is a quality of such awareness then one can enjoy a certain food or any other experience anew with a fresh quality each time one has it. It will be fresh because it will not have its roots in the past as such awareness of the activities of the "I" will prevent the enjoyment being turned into pleasure which is rooted in the past. This is a subject one must ponder over very deeply to grasp well, and such understanding of the ways of the "I" by observation is true meditation.

Pleasure is also inseparable from pain like the two sides of a coin. As long as the mind seeks pleasure, then pain is inevitable. Seeking of pleasure imprisons the mind into the limited walls of time whereas joy frees the mind from time in this present moment; therefore a quality of timeless living in the "now" naturally comes into being when one is actually joyful.

If one remembers one's earlier childhood or teenage times, then one can also remember how strongly rooted this enjoyment of life was; visiting one quite often. The main reason for this is the pleasure seeking mind was not as strong then. After a certain age, together with the conditionings of society, this pleasure seeking "self-centered" mind is strengthened in very subtle ways; therefore joy begins to move far away from us very silently without us being aware of her slow and gradual goodbye.

As explained above, joy, that true quality of happiness is something entirely different from pleasure, and it comes unexpectedly without seeking or planning. One cannot possibly seek or invite joy. Joy is like the breeze outside which will come as it will only if the house is well prepared with windows wide open. The very observation of the activities of the "I" which is self-knowing will slow down the movement of the "ego", and this very slowing down will be the opening of the windows for joy to come in. If there is lack of awareness of the activities of the ego then the ego will be wildly free to strengthen itself, and the stronger it gets the firmer the windows are closed.

Practical suggestions on joyful living:
-Be extremely aware of the activities of your mind in its very subtle ways of seeking pleasure.
-Do not seek or expect joy. Do not make any plans for it to come. Do not desire joy to come back again to your house if you are visited

by her because that very desire becomes the "I", the "ego" which shuts the windows of your house firmly for the breeze of joy to come in. Be rather disinterested to its comings and goings. Just make sure your house is always well prepared with windows wide open so that this breeze will find its way whenever it will. No need to mention the absolute necessity of having a healthy body to keep the windows wide open. Right vegetarian diet if you can, with a light body is greatly important. Being in relationship with nature as much as possible is also a major factor in opening the windows of your heart and soul. Also, being too ambitious for the worldly things such as wealth or fame obviously won't help the opening of the windows; on the contrary, they will have quite the opposite effect.

Letter#23
November 29, 2012

"You will feel your soul being undressed when the tender hands of love begin touching you. The many different masks on one's face will be removed, and the many different clothes which one is attached to will be ripped off one by one. Then, there will be a feeling of nothingness inwardly. Nothing to hold on to, nothing to be attached to, and nothing to lose; therefore no fear. And, when you are so totally naked inwardly, there will be a feeling of innocence. This will be the beginning of your immortal love story with the beloved."

Inward nakedness
We all have certain masks on our faces. Very rarely, we are absolutely truthful and totally innocent about who we really are. We always have something to be hidden inside from others. So, we never have this feeling of inward nakedness in which we have nothing to hide from others. Therefore, we are never in this state of innocence in our relationships. And, we naturally and easily become very truthful in such inward nakedness.

If we are not naked inwardly this way then all those things hidden in our consciousness must be observed and understood very carefully. We have so many images about ourselves like the "intelligent one" or the "beautiful one" etc. All these images are the factors which

51

prevent us from being naked inside. So, we must carefully and attentively be aware of such images by observing them very closely in our daily relationships. We must watch the response of our minds both when we are flattered or insulted. We can be flattered or insulted only if we have an image about ourselves. If we are in this state of inward nakedness with no image of ourselves at all, then neither flattery nor insult can touch us. And, we will never get hurt inwardly in such a state of the mind as it is only the image we built about ourselves which can get hurt. If we have no image of ourselves at all, then what is there left to get hurt?

One might rightly doubt whether it could at all be possible to live this way in a world in which almost everybody is somehow untruthful with extraordinarily cunning and clever minds. One can absolutely live this way in this world as this is something totally different from being stupidly naive. There is the supreme intelligence of love functioning through that quality of inward nakedness of the heart and the mind, and it is this intelligence of inner simplicity which is true wisdom; therefore such a mind will easily see the right way of dealing with the cunning and clever minds of today's world.

We are also attached to many different things like a boyfriend, girlfriend, furniture, car or the bank account etc. All such attachments must be wiped away since they become the things we hold on to, and as long as we hold on to something inwardly we can never be totally naked inwardly.

And, only in this quality of total inward nakedness we can know what love, joy and true happiness is.

Practical suggestions on inward nakedness:
-Be aware of the many different masks and images you have in your daily relationship.
-Be truthful.
- In the spiritual journey of climbing the mountain of truth, we must leave the entire inward burden behind so that we can feel light inwardly. Just like the simple action of getting undressed in a hot summer day, we should get undressed inwardly with that quality of simplicity without making it into another conflict of the spiritual

kind. Attachments are our inward clothes that we hold on to, and wise and true way of ending attachment with one simple action should be like taking our jacket out on a hot day without any complications involved. Just simply cut it off with one strike without the complications of time being involved. We do not take time and complicate the process of taking out our jacket; we simply take it out. We should also take out our inward jackets just like this with one simple action. If we can not abandon attachments with such simple action, then naturally we will find ourselves in a new conflict of detachment complication in which the mind will get lost again; whereas total freedom of the mind from any sense of conflict is the most essential thing on the path of wisdom. This quality of inward simplicity in action might be the only way to climb the mountain top in our spiritual journey, and when once we are undressed this way inwardly, then the light of the simplicity of inward nakedness will begin radiating.

Letter#24
November 30, 2012

"There is a point of maximum tension when a rope is stretched, and at that point there is strong vibrant energy. Similarly, we will be able to live with the highest form of mental energy when we live adventurously by pushing the limits as much as we can. Then, life itself becomes a great thrill. If one lives this way, then one becomes vital with full of energy instead of decay."

Living dangerously

We generally have a tendency to live with a feeling of psychological security. There is the physical security which is necessary, but is there such a thing as psychological security at all? At the physical level, the body must have security, but what is that inner security which we all crave for? Is inward security a reality that can be achieved by seeking, or is it just another illusion created by the mind in its futile attempts to escape suffering? Can there be a sense of permanent psychological security when there is death waiting for us at the end? Obviously not! That means we are looking for some temporary feeling of inward security while we are alive, but life will not leave us alone in our secure little isolated corner by throwing challenges on our path all the time because of its very dynamic nature. It is like a little fish trying to build a nest in a wild and mighty river in order to secure herself. All nests that she will be building will be destroyed by the river until this little fish realizes that the only true security comes with leaving herself into the hands of the river in total surrender which will then take her to an adventurous journey. Only the total inward freedom of love will provide us with that feeling of absolute inward security which we have been seeking all our lives. Can there be a way of living in which there is no seeking of such inward security? After all, what is there to be protected inside the skin other than the outer physical body itself? And, because we live with such demand for inner security, we cannot live adventurously which is the only way of true enjoyment in life.

Living dangerously does not imply any kind of danger for the physical body, but rather it implies a way of living which gives one a sense of thrill, and for that one must live like there is no tomorrow. A total denial of time as the past and the future is an absolute necessity as danger implies not knowing what the next moment shall bring. Then, the next moment always becomes a surprise of the unknown.

Also, all attachments must be destroyed to live this way. This is like moving with a wild river. The moment you hold on to anything you will move away from the river into the dirty stagnant waters. The river is vital with full of energy; whereas the other is dead. Attachment implies a demand for inward psychological security, and one must go beyond the demand for such inner security in order to move with the majestic river of life rather than becoming a dead living of the decaying waters.

In a way, the feeling of such danger is something like gambling with life. The best gamblers are the ones who play the game dangerously with no fear. For them, there is no next second in which they might lose the game. That feeling of 'no next second' wipes away fear entirely because fear can take its roots only in time. So, freedom from fear becomes the key here to live this way.

There must be a playful mood of pushing the things to their limits all the time just like the stretched rope with high tension. The art is all about stretching the rope to a further tension each time and getting closer to the breaking point but never breaking it. There is great joy in this way of living .There might naturally be certain risks in pushing the limits; but just like the gambler, one should invite life by inviting thrill rather than inviting death by seeking inward security. Then, life will begin dancing with us which will make us feel life as a living thing. Life will start being playful with us as well bringing in new challenges which will ascend the dance to the next level all the time. There is never a stop, no resting, but always moving further in this pushing of the boundaries. One should never be satisfied with the limit one has already gone beyond because life knows no limits. If one is satisfied with any limit which one has gone beyond, then at that very moment one will begin decaying in the stagnant waters. So one must always be aware whether one is asleep in the stagnant waters or fully awake in the vital river of life. This demands great attention to one's psychological state all the time. One must be fully awake all the time by watching the activities of one's mind.

Practical suggestions on living dangerously:
-Live like there is no next second.
-Be aware of your mind's demand for inward psychological security, and see the fact that such security is an illusion. It does not exist in reality. After all, there is death at the end of everything. Nothing is permanent.
-End attachments with ease.
-Push the limits all the time to a next level, and never get satisfied with the level you already got to.
-Have the spirit of a gambler a little bit in order to live and dance with life dangerously, and live your life with a spirit of danger and adventure without seeking any sense of psychological security like you are falling down a cliff. Do not seek anything to hold on to in this free fall because you will get terribly hurt if you attempt to get attached to something at high speed of such falling. Just enjoy the beautiful scenery each and every moment of this journey of free fall until you hit the ground. Life is all about fully enjoying this free fall until the very last second of hitting the ground. You will miss the whole point of living if you are concerned about the moment of

hitting the ground or what happens afterwards. Just enjoy the fall at the exact altitude you are without thinking about the lower or higher altitudes which implies living in the present.

Letter#25
December 02, 2012

"Life becomes routine and boring unless one gets into the mystical boat for a spiritual journey to the destination unknown."

The spiritual journey of life

Most of us tend to live an extremely superficial life only on the material platform of life. This way of living will inevitably take us to desperate unhappiness it does not matter how rich or successful we get on this material platform. This is an absolute fact.

If one were unfortunate enough to be the **private room** of a very famous or rich person, then one could witness their desperate sufferings behind the fake masks of happiness. One would see how lonely they are though they may be surrounded by many. Both the rich and the poor, the ordinary and the famous are bound to suffer if they live on the material platform only.

When we get bored living on this material platform only, we turn to seek a so called spiritual way of living, but generally the spiritual directions we choose to go are rather very limited and superficial as well. So, both living on the material platform or on the so called spiritual platform has very little meaning since they are both very superficial and limited, whereas there are great depths to be discovered in the true spiritual journey.

So, what then is the true spiritual journey about? Perhaps we can start by what it is not to have a better understanding. It is certainly not the repetition of certain mantras or following some gurus, saviors or masters it does not matter how so called holy they are. Even a truly enlightened person will be the barrier on your path if you accept that person as your spiritual authority to follow blindly. There is no particular temple like the church or the mosque, and there is no book to be worshipped. In true spirituality, heart is the only temple, and life is the worshipped. One does not belong to a particular organized religion. One must go beyond such religious or nationalistic divisions as the very essence of a spiritual life must be love, and love knows no such divisions among human beings.

To get into this boat, one must start questioning everything to find the truth of things, and what is most essential in this journey is self-knowledge. Self-knowledge is the very essence of a truly spiritual life. Without self-knowledge, there is no spirituality. Self-knowledge begins by observing oneself in daily relationship. One must learn to use relationship as a mirror to see oneself as one actually is. When you look at yourself in the mirror, you see what your face actually look like. If you have blue eyes, then you will see your blue eyes in the mirror. In the same way, can we see ourselves as we actually are in the mirror of relationship? Can we see our jealousy, anger, hatred, sympathy, sadness, loneliness etc. in this mirror as they actually are? Can we simply see without any attempt to change what we actually see into our idealization of what should be? When we look at our blue eyes in the mirror, we do not attempt to change them to green. We just look. That's it. In the same way, can we just be aware, and look at our inward qualities in this mirror of relationship? What we see in the mirror might not be pleasant, but can we just stay with what we see without any movement away from that fact of "what is"? Generally, we see something like jealousy which we do not like; therefore we want to move away towards a conceptual idea of "non-jealousy" which is an illusion. What is real is the fact of my jealousy, and I must understand this fact in order to be free from it, but the moment I move away from this fact to the idea of non-jealousy then I can never look at this fact very closely to understand. So, this movement from "what is" to "what should be" must come to an end totally. After all, how can one understand anything that one is trying to move away from by turning one's back to that thing? One must look at that thing closely face to face to really understand. What then? Then, there is only "what is" which is the "me" to be observed and understood. This is the only way to know oneself. If you move into an idea of "what you should be", then you are merely escaping from the fact of "yourself". As long as you run away from the actuality of yourself, you will never know yourself. Without knowing yourself this way, it is an impossibility to take this tremendous spiritual journey. Also, such process of self-knowledge is part of true meditation which will open a dimension of silence in the mind, and without coming into contact with this dimension one cannot possibly start one's inner journey. Such self-knowledge, once it begins, will take you to the deeper levels of understanding of love by understanding what love is not. This is true wisdom and your journey towards the unknown will begin from here. Then, life will not be a meaningless daily routine anymore. It will begin to have a significant meaning beyond the mere material. One will begin to live in a "mystical" world with enormous depths of beauty which cannot possibly be put into words.

So the absolute fact of life then is, 'there can never be true happiness on the material platform only, but there must be a well-balanced combination of the material and the spiritual world'.

Practical suggestions on the spiritual journey:
-Begin the journey of self-knowledge by seeing yourself as you actually are in the mirror of relationship. Do not try to change what you see in this mirror even if what you see is unpleasant. Just silently be aware of what you see which is what you actually are. Do not move away from what you actually are to any idea of what you should be. Just stay silently with what you actually are, and look.
-Question everything.
-Deny all spiritual authority. Be a light unto yourself by finding the truth of things for yourself. If you accept the spiritual authority of another, it does not matter who, then your journey will take you towards nothing but darkness only. You can walk on this spiritual path only with your own light of understanding. There are no absolute rules in the spiritual journey. There are no strict rights or wrongs, but rejection of all spiritual authority can be considered as the only law.
-Once a man asked a wise man what enlightenment was? The wise man said, "Imagine you have a stroke now, and you are dead. And, imagine your body came back to life after an hour or so by some miraculous rebirth fully conscious with all the physical senses fully awake; whereas your ego could not make it back to life again. That body of yours without your ego is your enlightened version". The

man looked quite puzzled and asked again, "How can my body survive and live without my ego"? The wise man replied, "Your body has the supreme universal intelligence within itself, and your ego is mere stupidity which blocks this intelligence, and your body without your ego will join the unitary movement of life. Then life itself will take care of your body effortlessly."

Letter#26
December 07, 2012

"You can't stop the challenges, but you can learn to surf."

Meeting the challenges of life

Challenges, if looked from another point of view, can be great teachers for our inner growth. Challenges that come to our lives will wake us up from a sleepy state of mind to an awakened one only if we meet them wisely. If we do not meet them this way, then they can be quite destructive as well. So, one must learn the art of surfing the waves of life.

What is a challenge actually? What do we mean by it? A challenge is something which disturbs our regular way of living in which we feel secure. For example, losing my job brings a challenge to my life to be faced. This challenge disturbs my routine of life which gives me a false feeling of safety. How should one face such a challenge? This is where the art of surfing begins. One can fall into a depression if one looks from one point of view; and from another point of view, one can wisely enjoy surfing the waves of life. So, two different people can meet the same challenge in two totally different ways.

In the wise way of meeting a challenge, one will immediately pay attention to oneself inwardly to see the effects of such challenge on the psyche. One will observe the responses of the mind to such a challenge. There can be fear, suffering, a feeling of being lost etc. The wise response will be seeing this challenge as a good opportunity to observe and to know oneself. Why? Simply because this challenge came as a teacher to show me that I am totally asleep in an illusion of safety. It also showed me that my inner balance and peace can very easily be destroyed, and this means I must study and learn about myself more. This challenge brought a new lesson to be studied now in the journey of self-knowledge, and the homework to be studied is fear and suffering. Every new challenge then, if met this way, will help us to climb the ladders of self-knowledge which is the only path of true wisdom.

By such approach, one will begin to meet the challenges of life with a playful mood rather than a depressive one. It will be similar like playing a video game then. Each challenge that comes to our path in life will imply a new level in the game. In order to get to the next level, one must be totally done with the current level. This means one must totally study and understand the effects of the challenge at this level. By understanding totally, one will be free from the fears and sufferings caused by the challenge of this magnitude at this level. One is now ready for the new level of challenges in life. New level of challenge will come to show us the hidden corners of our consciousness at much deeper levels, and this will naturally mean a further step into the great depths of wisdom in the journey of self-knowledge. Each new level reached will imply more awakening from the sleeping state of mind. Therefore, one will have more inward psychological energy which is the essence of a happy life. The more one is awakened in such self-study, the less one is capable of inner suffering; and a mind which reaches the ultimate level is totally awakened and it is totally free from suffering. In such totally awakened state, there is no such thing as a challenge anymore that can cause any sense of pain. Such a mind just surfs the waves of life with great enjoyment of living.

So, such challenges, if one knows the art of surfing, will shed great light unto our path of self-knowledge which is the only way to wisdom. And the very same challenges can also bring darkness to our lives if they are not met wisely this way. So, do not be scared of challenge itself, but rather meeting them without wisdom.

One must also go into the question of what a challenge is as well. If we are happy causelessly which is the only true happiness anyway, then can any so called challenge disturb a truly happy heart? Challenges are generally destructive and disturbing because they often threaten the causes of our so called happiness, but if our happiness is causeless then what is there to be threatened at all? Causeless happiness has one and only one cause, and that is very living itself. The happiness that is born out of being alive and breathing on a marvelous planet called earth is the only true happiness. Such happiness implies naturally no attachments to anything. Then, the only needs become proper food, clothes and shelter and nothing else. Until one knows the immense inward strength of such causeless happiness, one will be vulnerable to so called challenges, and with that quality of happiness, what is called challenge otherwise will just become a thrilling wave to be surfed.

Practical suggestions on meeting the challenges:
-Begin to see each new challenge of life as a teacher who is pointing out the next level on the path of wisdom rather than feeling depressed.
-Have a playful mood while meeting the challenges just like playing a video game. Get totally done with the current challenge of your life, and life will open the next level of game for you. Having said that, of course life is not a game, and the word 'game' is used here rather as a metaphor as life is a much too serious thing than that of a game; but this metaphor is used only to better explain the wise way of dealing with the challenges in life. What is the other way of dealing with challenges anyway? For sure this way of playful sprit is wiser than getting depressed with the enormous challenges life might throw on our path.

Letter#27
December 14, 2012

"Identification with the body gives us a false sense of separateness from the rest of the world. This feeling of separateness is the root cause of suffering. The ending of such identification is the beginning of a feeling of unity in which suffering cannot take place."

Identification with the body
Are we aware of the fact that we are so strongly identified with our bodies? We identify ourselves with many different things such as our

car, our house, bank account etc. The process of identification gives us a sense of false inward security and strength. If we do not identify ourselves with one thing or another, we are scared of being nothing inwardly. Therefore, we want to be something through this identification process. To be something outwardly, such as being a doctor, is all right, but why do we have to be something inwardly at all? One can be a doctor, and at the same time, one can have no images of oneself psychologically. One will function as a doctor in the physical outer world, but one won't build up an image of a doctor in the psychological inner world. Such images can be the good doctor, intelligent doctor, successful doctor, good looking doctor...etc

So, can one live with no psychological identifications at all? After all, what is the need for such identifications anyway? One might need to be something in the physical world like being a doctor for survival, but is there any need at all to be somebody inwardly? There is no need at all. So, why do we continue this process of identification which will inevitably cause suffering? For example, if I have an image of myself as the intelligent one, then I am bound to get hurt if somebody thinks I am stupid. This process of identification is merely strengthening the ego and making one vulnerable to being hurt. So, one must be extremely aware of this identification process at very subtle deeper levels of consciousness as well as the superficial ones.

As explained above, we have great tendency to identify ourselves with many different things, but one type of identification is totally different from all others, and that is the identification with the body. That is the ultimate identification, because the "self" or the "ego" takes its shelter there. Therefore, there is a qualitative difference between the identification with the body and the identification with any other object. The "I" says "my car, my money, my business...etc", and the "I" also says "my body". The feeling of "my body" is qualitatively different from all other "my things". Therefore, when we look at the world with our physical eyes, we unconsciously divide the material world into two parts qualitatively, and that is "the body" and "all other things". This, in fact, is an optical illusion. The body is no different from any other object in the world qualitatively. It is the body. That is it. For an outside observer who is looking from the objective space, "your body" is no different from any other material object. It is "a" material object in the world, and it is part of the material world, but when we look at the world, the eyes see the body and the other objects as two different things qualitatively. This optical illusion must end.

An example can probably make it easier to understand this optical illusion of the qualitative division. The virtual video games technology is very high now. Imagine yourself in one of these very high tech video games, and let's say you are given a perfect virtual body. When your eyes look at the world in the game, is there any such qualitative separation like "your virtual body" and "your virtual car"? No. There is no such division. They are all part of the same electronic screen, and your virtual body is no different from your virtual car qualitatively. But, when you start playing the game, the game might get very exciting, and you might forget you are in a game at certain times. The moment you forget you are in the video game, identification with your virtual body begins. You even get very scared when somebody points a gun towards you in the game. But, what is the truth? The truth is you are in a video game and the virtual body is a part of the game. It is not something qualitatively different. One sees the whole of the game as one indivisible picture at the beginning before identification with the virtual body, and one sees the game from a center of the "I" after identification. What is the difference? The difference is; 'seeing the whole is seeing the truth, and perceiving through division is the optical illusion.'

Of course, life is not a video game, but similarly, can we see life as an indivisible whole which really is simply seeing the truth? For this, division must come to an end, because there is either the undivided whole or the division. The factor which makes up the "center", and therefore the division, is the "I" or the "ego". When the eyes look at the world without this center of the "I", then the whole which is the truth will naturally be perceived. This can be possible only if the identification process with the body ends. The spiritual awakening is basically about this waking process from the dream of identification with the body. It is like your friend telling you that it is just a game; when you are very scared at an exciting moment of a video game. If you are too identified and attached to the game, then you are asleep in reality. When your friend shakes and awakens you to the fact that it is just a game, then you are back to reality. Spiritual awakening is quite similar to this process. We are asleep in life with all our identifications, attachments, pains, sufferings, pleasures, addictions etc. And through the process of observation and awareness, we wake up to the reality. This is simply what spiritual awakening is about. Spiritual awakening has nothing to do with all the complications of the so called spiritual books or gurus. They are confused in the world, and they carry their confusion to a so called spiritual world. Spirituality, if there are any complications, is not spirituality at all. Spirituality must be simple and intelligent. After all, as explained above it is merely a process of being awakened from an illusion. It is not about all those strange so called mystical experiences or nirvanas...etc. Simple intelligence which is the only wisdom is the key on this path of spiritual awakening.

Practical suggestions on identification with the body:
-Imagine yourself playing a very high tech video game with a virtual body. The virtual body is not different from the virtual car in the game. There is no real feeling of "my car" or "my body" since it is just a video game. Live your life this way. See it as "the body" instead of "my body", and "the car" instead of "my car".
- Imagine you could take off your body just like you take off your clothes, and this implies freedom from the identification with the body. When you have time in a quiet place, try to imagine what it would feel like to take off the body. And, what remains after taking off the body?

Letter#28
December 19, 2012

"Narrow your 'one life' down to 'one moment', and live in that moment as if it is the only moment just like the only life you have."

One life, one moment
Look at your life as a whole from birth till death. It is "one life". There was no yesterday for you on the day you were born, and there will be no tomorrow on the day you die. So, this "one life" time space does not have a past or future. "One life" may imply 50,60,70 or 80

years of time distance, but it is a time distance like 1 day or 1 week. Using the same concept of "one life", we can narrow it down to 1 week or 1 day, and live as if it is the only week or the only day, just like the only life we have. The ultimate spiritual target is to narrow it down to one moment, and live for the moment like it is the only moment without any previous or next moment. Living for the day, in comparison to living for the week, implies more presence in the "now", and living for the moment is the ultimate presence in the "now" and the peak of spiritual awakeness.

Living in the "now" has unfathomable depths as there is never a final arrival. The more one goes deeper into the present moment, the more the present moment expands its borders. It is an endless journey in the timelessness of the "now", and there is great joy in the discovery of the unknown depths of the present. Life will have a true meaning only when one begins living this way. Otherwise, it will always be a repetitively boring thing within the limitations of the known. One must cross the borders of the known to the unknown in order to begin living fully, and this is only possible by mastering this art of dancing with the present moment. This dance is basically between "thinking" and "awareness of thinking". Thinking is the movement away from the present moment into the river of time, and awareness is coming back to the present. This is not "you" being aware because "you" are the past, therefore part of time. This is a quality of awareness in which there is a watchfulness of the movement of thinking like you are watching the sunset on a far horizon. You just watch the sunset in silence. You do not want to alter the way the sun sets, nor do you judge it; but you just watch it calmly with a sense of tranquility. Thought stops its entire activity when one watches the beauty of a sunset, and there is only a quality of quiet watchfulness. Imagine your physical eyes watching such an outward scene in nature, and simply turn your eyes which are watchful this way to the inner scene where thought movement takes place. This should be the quality of watchfulness of the movement of thinking, and this quality itself is awareness. When thought begins moving awareness stops, and when awareness is back then thought stops, and the dance continues with an ever increasing rhythm to the point of a totally new dimension of silence coming into being where there is only the dancing of life itself left without a 'dancer as the I'.

In order to start this dance, there must be a deep understanding of the relationship between the ego and time. The ego or the "I" has its roots in the past. It is built up by the memories of the past. Without memory, it cannot exist. For example, at the age of 25, the "I" is made up of 25 years of memory accumulation. And, the experiences of each year add to the "I" and shape its characteristics. These experiences can be hurt, happiness, betrayal etc. So the "I" is basically made and shaped by a bundle of memories accumulated through time. The very process of such accumulation gives us the false illusory feeling of time as a movement from the past to the future. The "I" looks back and sees the past, and it looks ahead and sees the future, and it thinks it is in a movement towards the future; whereas in reality, there is only the present moment. The physical movement of the objects is the physical time. This physical movement is from here to there or from LA to New York, and it has a physical direction like from east to west. That is it. There is no movement like from the past to the future. The very existence of the "I" is creating this illusion. There is only the present moment which contains all time, and there is the physical movement of the objects in this present moment. That is all, and this physical movement becomes the chronological or the physical time of the clocks. This physical time is the only time, and it is relative to the physical movement in the universe. There is no absolute time which is independent from the physical movement in the universe, but we think there is such a time which is a movement from the past to the future. This time movement from the past to the future exists only in human mind. In reality, there is no such time movement; therefore this psychological movement is an illusion which is at the root of entire human conflict.

So, the ego is the past. And it projects a future by its hopes, desires, goals, fears etc. This means as long as the ego is there, one is bound to live in time, but never live in the present moment. There is no such a thing as the "I" living in the present moment because the "I" is the past, and that past can never touch the present moment. It is like two parallel lines which can never meet. The "I" talks about living in the present moment, but it has very little meaning. The mind will be living in the present moment only when the past stops meeting the present; which means the "I" should come to an end.

There are certain rare moments in our lives when we feel a true sense of joy. At that moment, the "I" somehow ends for a second or so leaving the mind freed from time; therefore it touches the present moment, but the "I" comes back next second by saying "what a joy it was". So, to live in the present moment, the "I" must end. For this, one must go deep to observe and understand the ways of the "I" which are extremely subtle. Such observation is part of meditation and self-knowledge. The more one goes deeper and deeper into the present moment, the more one life becomes one timeless moment of eternity.

Practical suggestions on one life, one moment:

-Be aware of your lack of attention to what you are doing. You might be walking, talking, eating or washing the dishes. Our minds generally have a very strong tendency to wander away in time thinking about something else while we are doing a certain thing; therefore the attention of the mind gets divided, and we never really do what we are doing with full attention.

-Do not label certain activities in your daily life as unimportant. For example, you might not like waiting for the bus or spending time in the toilet, and you might see them as unimportant. But, what is ultimately more important is to stay in the present moment fully all the time, because only then we become one with life and be happy "only" for being "alive". So, when you are waiting for the bus, wait for it by staying in the moment with full attention to things around you passing by.

-Once in a while, do "living in the present" meditation. Just choose a day or a few hours some time, and within that period of time live like your past and future is totally removed. After this temporary period ends, you can come back to your normal life, but just for a little period of time, live like there is no past or future but that moment, hour or day only. Once you start doing this meditation you will see more and more you will begin to live totally in the present moment naturally at other times as well, and you will love it because there is great joy of living in it.

-End everything psychologically at the end of each day. Do not carry your anger, hurt ... etc. to the next day because their continuity prevents you to live in the present moment fully.

Memo Ozdogan

-Be aware of unnecessary thinking. We sometimes waste hours and days thinking about a very simple thing which could be properly handled with a few minutes of clear thinking that comes out of a peaceful mind. Excessive thinking will prevent us from living totally in this present moment because we can't be totally attentive to the "now" while we are lost in endless thoughts.

-End attachments with ease without conflict. Attachment has its roots in the past; therefore it blocks you from being fully in this present moment.

-Imagine you were born on another planet like Mars, and that you came to earth for a holiday only for one week. How would you live on earth then? Would you not get mesmerized by the immense beauty of life itself only, and would you not enjoy the experience of life with its great beauty? Wouldn't it be like an ecstatic dream? Of course, after a week the problems of living we currently have would begin taking their roots soon. If it is only a week, then we would live like a guest to enjoy it fully. The problems start only when we stick to it to be the owner of the house rather than staying as a guest just to enjoy. So, can we live on this earth as a guest ready to leave any time rather than taking deep roots? And, the absolute fact is that we are nothing but just guests on this earth, it does not matter how long we live. As long as we want to take deep roots, there will be eternal conflict between the fact of being a guest and the desire to be the owner. So, can we live on this earth as a guest all the time like that very first 1 week of arrival to earth for the first time? Not being attached to anything; therefore ready to leave any time as a guest would. Seeing the beauty of life anew with fresh eyes every morning, just like the first time of seeing life at that very first arrival to earth for a week of holiday. Meditate upon why we can't live our weeks like that very first week.

Letter#29
December 20, 2012

"Life is an empty canvas which is given to us at birth, and the secret meaning of life is hidden in how this canvas will be painted."

The canvas of life

Painting title: Today
Artist: The lover of life

Think of your life, from birth till death, as a big painting canvas. It is an empty canvas at birth, and it is being painted by each moment passing by. This canvas is made up of very limited edition pieces which are the days of our life. Even if you have all the money of the world, you cannot buy an extra piece to paint on. So, it is strictly limited edition by the number of the days we have in our lives. And, each morning we are given a piece from this canvas which we call today. This piece is the only real piece to paint on. The piece called as yesterday has already been painted, and the piece that is called as tomorrow is not in our hands now; therefore it cannot be painted. So, naturally, we should give our full attention to this piece we have in our hands and start painting on it. This is the normal and healthy thing to do, but we as human beings are either concerned about the piece called yesterday or the piece called tomorrow. We do not even carefully look at this piece which is in our hands **at present**, and which is the only real piece from the canvas as well. We are more concerned about tomorrow's piece and this is an illusion, because the only piece which we can paint on is today. Unless this piece is given full attention, it will be wasted. And, because our minds are either in the future or in the past, it is mostly wasted. Unfortunately, this means our lives are being wasted simply because we are caught up in an illusion of time which blocks us from seeing the reality of today, and because of this illusion we waste a beautiful piece of canvas which is given to us each day. Time is like a veil that is put in between our eyes and the canvas piece of today which is in front of our eyes. Instead of making a beautiful picture with attention and love by using each piece we are given, we just make some meaningless and confused drawings because we are like a blind person who does not actually see the piece to paint on.

The meaning and the purpose of life is hidden in how this canvas will be used. At the end, it can be a wasted canvas full of confusion, or it can be made into a spectacular masterpiece of the art of painting. A great painter like Leonardo da Vinci gives full attention to each single "meeting" of his brush with the canvas, because he instinctively knows the secret of the beauty of the totality which will come at the end is hidden in the quality of each of these "meetings" of that very moment. He is not concerned about what will come at the end, nor does he have a purpose of an end beauty, because that very purpose which is in the future will become the veil which will prevent him to give full attention to the meetings of **now**. The beauty of each such meeting will determine the total beauty of the painting called life, and this meeting of the brush and canvas in the painting of life is called today, or this present moment.

So, how much attention and love we give to each moment and to each day is extremely important, because it determines the quality of the painting named life. This is the secret of life. You have one and only one canvas, and you can paint only now. Not tomorrow or yesterday, but now. Only then you will master the art of living; then you will be the artist, the lover of life who is painting his or her masterpiece with a title as **today**.

Practical suggestions on painting the picture of life:
-Give your full attention to what you are doing in any present moment. Don't label what you are doing as important or not important, but give full attention and love, because there is no such thing as the important or the unimportant part in the beauty of the final picture. Each single part of the painting has its own importance, and total beauty of the painting depends on the attention given to any part. So, give full attention to whatever you are doing in the present moment, because any present moment has its own unique place in the total picture of life.

Letter#30
December 25, 2012

Secret key meditation
First, close your eyes, and sit down in a quite environment alone for about 2 to 3 minutes, and just relax. Make up an imaginary key in your mind. Make sure it will be a beautiful one that you will love. This key will be your imaginary secret key to open the door to the light of joyful living.

A human body is composed of a physical body and a psychological self, me or the ego. Let's call it, 'the self', for the moment. So, there is a physical body, and there is a spiritual or psychological entity called 'the self'. Now, make up an imaginary spiritual body for 'the self'. This spiritual body can be identical to the physical body, but make sure you feel like there are two different bodies now; one physical, and one spiritual body for 'the self'. This imaginary spiritual body will have arms, legs, hands etc. all controlled by 'the self'.

Now, hold your secret key with your spiritual body's hand. Feel you are holding it with your spiritual hand. The physical body should be motionless during the entire meditation session. Move your imaginary secret key through your physical skull into the brain by using your spiritual hand which is capable of going through the skull. Now, your 'secret key' is in your mind just like 'the self' in your mind. Try to 'actually' touch 'the self' with your secret key just like a real key touches a point on your physical body. Remember, 'the self' is 'you' in the mind. So, touching 'the self' with your secret key means, in fact, touching 'you' in the mind. If you can really make your secret key touch 'you' by truly feeling it, then that will be the moment of total self-awareness through which life energy can flow into your whole being. Before the ending of each session, feel the unity of the 'secret key' and 'you' in that touch of the two, and now feel that there is only your secret key in the center of your mind with no 'you' anymore because the touch ended the illusion of the self center.

Try to do this every day preferably in the mornings. You will start feeling a sense of freshly new space and quietness taking place in your mind beginning from the the first session, but if you continue doing it for a while then the effects will be much stronger day by day. The whole session must be at least 10 minutes in a quite environment. Longer is better if you can.

The most important thing for the secret key meditation is that you must really feel each step like it is actually happening. And, these steps are:

1. Making up your imaginary secret key

2. Actual feeling of having a separate imaginary spiritual body for 'the self', and the feeling of holding your secret key with the hand of your spiritual body

3. The secret key going deep into your mind through your physical skull

4. The secret key touching 'you' in the mind

5. The secret key touch energizing the body and the mind

Please do not forget that the real secret key which will open the door to the light of joyful living comes with understanding and self-knowledge. That is the main thing. The above secret key meditation is just a practical exercise designed to open some new space in the mind through which the mind can receive life energy, but it is not the major thing which will give you the ultimate spiritual realization.

Letter#31
December 29, 2012

"The truth of oneself will be perceived only when one observes oneself with total objectivity free from any sense of judgment."

Observe yourself like you are not you

The real key for spiritual growth lies in the observation of oneself in the mirror or relationship, but the quality of the observation is the most important and critical thing for this key to be functional. How is one to observe? What should be the quality of the observation so that out of such observation one gains genuine self-knowledge which is the essence of a true spiritual life.

Can the observation be with no judgments at all? For instance, let's say jealousy is perceived through this observation; can we look at the fact of jealousy without saying it is right or wrong, and without trying to change it into an idea of non-jealousy? Can we just stay with the fact and look at it? This can be possible only if there is a quality of observation in which there is no division as the observer who is "you", and the observed which is the fact of 'jealousy'. This means a pure and %100 objective observation of the fact of "what is". The "I" or the "ego" can never be %100 objective especially when it is looking at its own qualities such as its jealousy. That is why, we can look at many things quite objectively, but hardly and rarely can we look at our own selves with such objectivity. Such %100 sense of pure objectivity is needed though, because only then, the truth of what one actually is will be seen in the mirror of relationship without any distortion. This is real self-knowledge, because only then you will begin to know yourself truly as you actually are; and not as who you should be. One might see jealousy, lack of love or hatred, but one will know the truth of oneself, and this perception will have its own action on what is perceived. The very perception of one's truth will set one free.

Most of us can never look at ourselves as explained above, simply because the ego that is observing cannot observe itself this way with pure objectivity. This is also the reason why human beings always blame the other in relationship. We cannot clearly see our jealousies or other qualities of ourselves as easy as we see such qualities in others. So, the critical thing then is; 'can I observe myself like I am not me'? It sounds a bit strange, but it is quite interesting if one goes into this issue deeply, and one should because this is the only way one can truly know oneself. Without such self-knowing, there is no spirituality.

Just watch yourself like "you" are not there as the observer. It is simply a silent quality of observation in which the "me" with all its chattering, judgments etc. is not there anymore. Look at yourself from a silent and deep presence of consciousness. If you do not find it weird, you can think of it as the "dead you" watching the "living you". What is meant by this metaphor? The metaphor of the "dead you" used in the sense that you cannot do anything. You cannot judge, talk, make noise etc. This is like you are watching yourself outside of your body from the deep stillness of a silent presence of consciousness. Then, you will be able to observe yourself like you are not you, but rather as the silent presence; therefore this will be a pure and %100 objective observation through which true self-knowing will naturally be flourishing.

Practical suggestions on observing yourself:

-Observe yourself like you are observing the sunset. Just look without any judgments of the right or the wrong; like the sunset which is neither right nor wrong. It is simply there to look. That's it.

-Your physical eyes are reading this now, and there is also the 'reader' in this process. Who is that 'reader'? Can you turn inward, and look at that reader 'now'? Can you see the reader clearly? Who is looking at the reader, and is that looker different from the reader? Can the 'reader', the 'looker' and 'you' be one single entity? And, if that is so, then the question becomes; 'can you look at 'you' now'? But, then isn't it again 'you' trying to look at 'you' which is impossible? Can there be a quality of looking at you without you? And, can that quality be freedom?

- Play games with your ego by inviting certain situations in which the ego will feel ashamed, desiring, angry, fearful, lustful, humiliated, etc. Basically, invite all the emotions and feelings, and watch the ego from all these different angles. For instance, if you have a friend who looks down on you, try spending some time with that person as a spiritual exercise, and watch the ego in its reactions. Since you have deliberately invited such an occasion awareness will be growing on the background; therefore you won't get harmed. Try pushing it more to the limits each time with greater awareness, and you will see this will help you to grow so much inwardly. After some time, the ego will begin liking this spiritual exercise, because it will soon realize it gets great strength by going beyond itself to the higher levels of knowledge through such exercise. Be aware of this too. Then, the ego will say, "Who is being aware? It is also me". Be aware of this as well. Just watch, and you will find yourself in laughter sometimes in this fun game with the ego, and that laughter will be the signs of joyful wisdom coming into existence unexpectedly and unknowingly at the moments of watchfulness without a watcher anymore as the ego.

Letter#32
January 1, 2013

"The very question of 'Do I really love?' will be the guide which will shed light upon one's spiritual path."

Is this real love?

This simple question of "is this real love?" can take one to the path of love, if it is asked and pursued seriously. Apply this question to your daily relationships with your husband, wife, children etc., and ask yourself this question at the end of each day. One must be very earnest, sincere and honest to oneself when one puts this question. Otherwise, it will have very little meaning. Let's say you met your friend today and spent some time together. Put this question to yourself after meeting your friend, and see whether you really love your friend, or you love what you get from your friend either in some subtle or obvious ways. These can be psychological pleasure of possessing your friend, using your friend as an escape from your loneliness and boredom, personal or business expectations, sexual pleasure etc. If there is seeking of any kind of benefit from a relationship, then love cannot exist in that relationship. One can benefit from a relationship naturally and unintentionally, and there is nothing wrong with that, but if one is deliberately looking for any kind of benefit physically or psychologically, then there is no love.

So, this question will shed light upon one's path of love. It is a great spiritual tool if used seriously and honestly. This tool will show "what love is not" very clearly, and the very seeing of "what love is not" is love being unfolded. Love cannot be approached positively as there is no path to it, but it can be approached by the negation of "what love is not". Each time one uses this tool, and asks this question to oneself seriously and honestly, the light of love will begin radiating more intensely. Also, be very critical of yourself when you put this question. A well balanced critical awareness of oneself is the key for this question to take you for a joyful journey into the depths of the path of love. It is a very practical tool, and you will see its spiritual effects in your life from the moment you begin using it. Your awareness of love will get stronger immediately. Just, put this question and look. There is the area of "what love is not" in you, and together with this question another area which is the "awareness of what love is not" will begin growing more and more, and the "awareness of what love is not" is love itself.

Why is love so important? It is important because love, peace and happiness are inseparable on the true spiritual path, and one cannot come alone by itself without the others. Love is the essence of a truly spiritual life. Most of the new age spiritual movements emphasize more on happiness which they think will come by success, but love is absolutely the essence. Without love, your spirituality will be nothing but entertainment of spiritual kind which is exactly same like being entertained by football. Can you think of happiness without love in one's heart? It will only be a so called happiness which is based on the material things and successes of the world, and surely that cannot be genuine happiness. So, love must come first, and when the light of love begins to show itself, joy and peace will naturally come in with that light.

Unfortunately, the word "love" has already lost its original true meaning. It is being used for many different purposes like the love of one's country, one's husband or wife, one's bank account etc. And, some even go further talking about the "love" of killing.

What is love in its truest sense? Shouldn't it imply an action totally free from any sense of self-centeredness? If there is any sense of selfishness in my action, obvious or subtle, then can this be the action of love? To put it in another way, if there is any "because" in my love, then is it real love? If I love her "because" of anything, then do I really love her, or do I love what that "because" gives me? This will bring us also to another question; which is, 'can there be love with any conditions, or love must be totally unconditional'? Unconditional love does not mean giving stupidly though. Such love has its own extreme quality of intelligence, and it deals with people properly by using this intelligence.

If the action of love is totally free from any sense of self-centeredness, then can there be any action of the "I" which is totally free from selfishness of any kind, Or by its very nature, any action of the "I" must be self-centered? The "I" is the self-center, and any action of the "I" must be self-centered then, mustn't it? If this is so, then one can say; 'the "I" can never truly love'. Then, for one to love, the "I" must end with all its clever and subtle activities. One must go very deep to see the very root of the "I", and end it there at the very origin. Love must be timeless, and this means freedom from time which is the "I" with its roots in the past. This requires great deal of self-knowledge, watchfulness, observation and attention to the activities of the "I", and this process of self-study is part of true meditation.

When the "I" ends, then perhaps there is love, and that love is not mine or yours. It is love which is free from "the me" or the "the you". There is no "I love you" then, but perhaps there is love in which there is no division anymore as "the me" and "the you", and perhaps there is unity then that might be the only true quality of love.

Practical suggestions on 'Is this real love?' :
-Try to ask yourself this question as often as possible in your daily relationships, and you will see the more you ask and pursue it sincerely and seriously until the very end, the more light will be shed on your spiritual path.
-Be very closely aware of the activities of the ego in all its obvious and subtle forms. The ego always looks for a benefit for itself from all relationships. Such benefit seeking can be extraordinarily subtle to be seen easily; therefore one must be very awake to the activities of the ego the way one would be awake if one is in a small room with the most venomous snake of the world. If there is any kind of benefit seeking in your relationships, then love cannot exist, because love is unconditional.
-See the fact that love and the 'I' or 'the ego' cannot share the same room at the same time. The ending of one is the beginning of the other.

Letter#33
January 7, 2013

"The chances of joy touching one when one loses a job is higher than when one lives with the fear of losing it."

Thought makes things look worse than they actually are
There are certain facts of this world, and things might not be all right all the time in life. We might go through certain difficulties such as a divorce, losing a job, losing a loved one etc. These are the facts of

life. Can we meet these facts without the complication of thought which builds the network of fear based on these facts?

There are two things which must be separated for clear observation to take place. One thing is the actuality of the thing itself, and the second is the picture thought makes of this actuality. And, the picture made by thought is never the actual thing itself. For example, think of a person called X, and let's say X has hundred friends. All of these hundred people will have a different picture of X in their minds made by their thinking mechanism, but none of these pictures will be the actual truth of X though all will think they have the absolutely true picture. There cannot be hundred different pictures of X which are all true. So, the picture that thought makes of anything is never the actual; therefore these two must be distinguished well for clarity of seeing.

In the same way, thought makes pictures of certain possible facts which might take place in our lives. For instance, we might lose our job one day. There are two things here again which must be distinguished. First, the actuality of the possibility of me losing my job, and the picture thought makes of this possible actuality of my life. Let's think of a shock scale of this actuality from level 0 to level 10; ten being the worst case scenario that can take place in my life. Let's say losing a job will be positioned at level 3 or 4 on this scale, considering there are much worse things with greater shock in life such as having a serious health problem. So, from the objective point of view, losing my job is positioned at levels 3 or 4, and this is the objective actuality. After all, it is a job that is being lost, and it is not the end of the world. One can always find a new one. Now, the very nature of thought often has the tendency to distort this actuality by falsely showing it much worse than it actually is. Therefore, the picture of losing my job which is made by thought will be positioned between levels 7 and 10 on this shock scale; whereas in objective reality it should have been positioned at levels 3 or 4 as explained above. So, what actually happened here? Thought functioned as a delusionary magnifier, and caused one a lot of unnecessary suffering by magnified fear effect. For some people, even something which should be positioned at level 1 on the objective shock scale can move further up to level 10 on the picture which thought made of the same thing. This is the extreme case, but it is true. So, the level of deviation on the scale changes from person to person. The wise is the one who can live with zero deviation on this scale, and this is only possible when thought totally stops making a picture of an actuality in one's life. Then, one will live with only the undistorted fact itself; therefore one will be able to meet the fact directly without any picture of the fact made by thought which is fear, and this will naturally enable one to see the facts as they actually are.

This quality of seeing the things of life as they **actually** are, is wisdom. So, quite often, thought has this tendency to make things look worse than they actually are; and unfortunately the 'optimistic' approach is suggested by the experts to cure this specific disease of thought; never realizing the fact that so called optimism is still the distortion of the fact in another direction; hence preventing one to see the thing as it actually is. In that sense, neither optimism nor pessimism has any place in the wise art of seeing the thing as it actually is. Of course, hopelessness which is the opposite of hope of optimism is not suggested here though; but what is implied here rather is that when there is wisdom of actual perception of the thing as it is, then there is no question of hope or hopelessness; optimism or pessimism, but rather a direct factual perception of that thing of our life which is the supreme intelligence of wisdom with its proper action that will be the real cure.

The chances of joy touching one when one loses a job is higher than when one lives with the fear of losing it, and this can be applied to any other fear. Joy can come only when one lives 100% factually; which means no fear. With the fact itself, there is no fear. Fear comes in only when thought starts making a picture of the fact. If there is no picture, then there is only the fact to be observed. Fact is never fearful. It is just the fact. So, one must be extraordinarily aware of thought process creating a picture of the fact, and one must separate the fact from the picture made by thought. This understanding is part of meditation.

Practical suggestions on thought making things look worse than they actually are:

-Be aware of thought's subtle operations that make things look much worse than they actually are.

-Be neither pessimistic nor optimistic about the certain challenging things which might possibly take place in your life. Be factual by seeing how hard life could be for you if that thing actually takes place, and stay with this fact. Be constantly aware of thought's tendency to make this thing look much worse than its actual magnitude. For example, the actual level of suffering which will be caused by a simple headache or a cancer disease is entirely different. But, if thought begins to play with it then it can even turn a simple headache into some kind of paranoia. In the same way, thought can make certain things which might take place in our lives look much worse. If we are going to suffer, let's suffer at the objective level of actuality which is a simple headache, and let's not suffer an amplified pain effect caused by the simple headache being turned into an illusionary pain of a greater magnitude by the thinking mechanism.

Letter#34
January 17, 2013

"We will begin to live fully only when we surrender totally to the river of life, and begin moving with it towards the vast ocean, because the very meaning of life is hidden in the river joining the ocean."

The river of life
Life is like a vast mighty river flowing with great vitality, and this is the beauty of life. Shall we move with the vital flow, or shall we look for a safe little inwardly isolated corner by the side of the river which is full of stagnant water rather than the dynamic river? This question is basically about being a dead living or living life to its fullest with a spirit that invites adventure all the time.

Most people seek inward psychological security. This seeking of security can be understood at the food, clothes and shelter level which is needed for the protection of the psychical body. But, apart from this, is there any other kind of psychological security at all? The fact is there is no such security. The seeking of such security is unreal. It is an illusion. After all, there is death at the end of everything, and this implies there is no permanent security. Also, whatever inward psychological security we might have in this stagnant pool we build for ourselves can easily be destroyed by the wildly moving river any time; and it will be destroyed because life constantly throws us new challenges.

What happens if one does not seek any inward psychological security at all? The physical body must be secured, but apart from the physical body, what is there to be secured? It is the 'self' or the 'me' or the 'ego' which desires security, isn't it? If the physical body is not secured, one's life might be harmed; so it must be secured. But, if there is no seeking of any psychological security, then the 'self' won't be secured, and what happens if it is not secured? Nothing. Life will continue as long as the physical body is there. Also, apart from the food, clothes and shelter, that inner psychological security is a very relative thing which changes greatly from person to person. For the person in Africa who is fighting starvation, that security means some food for today to survive; for another who is wealthy, that security might mean another billion on top of the one he has already accumulated. This implies, there is no absolute feeling of inward security. Therefore, wisdom demands not to seek any inward security at all. The security of the physical body is important, and that is all. Seeking psychological security is simply seeking the impossible, because it does not exist in reality. And, the fake feeling of inward security which we find after seeking for a long time will inevitably be destroyed by the dynamic challenges of life sooner or later anyway. The moment we build such a house of mental security which we depend on for our inner stability; fear of losing that also builds up simultaneously, and the conflict begins. So, why not live without seeking any psychological security to depend on at all? Wouldn't it be much wiser, simpler and more peaceful to live this way? This does not necessarily mean getting accustomed to the feeling of inward insecurity with its suffering though, but rather when one begins a serious spiritual search, in that journey one will begin to feel truly secure when the light of love begins to shine within. And, this might be the only true and absolute psychological security.

What happens if one sees the fact of psychological security being an illusion? One simply stops seeking such inward security in any direction. This means; one leaves the little stagnant pool and jumps into the living river of life. Different from the stagnant waters, this river can be a wild one at times, and that is the beauty of it. There is no psychological security in the river. Flowing freely with the river and enjoying it without seeking any security, in itself, is the absolute feeling of security. So, if one does not seek any psychological security at all, then one will feel totally secure with a feeling of inner liberation. The very seeking of security itself creates the feeling of insecurity, and the moment one stops seeking it, this feeling of insecurity comes to an end.

The very meaning of life is flowing with the vital river. This means living dangerously with an adventurous spirit. When one lives this way, life strangely comes to the help of one in many different and unexpected ways. This help can come through the person we meet by coincidence, or through a facebook post...etc., and our lives can change totally. But for this to take place, one must be in the river. Then, the river will take us where it will. There will be thrill in the river; therefore one will feel alive.

Change is probably the only thing that does not change in the world. Non-acceptance of the fact of changes in life means great struggle and waste of lots of precious life energy. It is like trying to walk against the current of a majestic river, and get destroyed by it. The very nature of life is constant change like this river. Trying to walk against it, or trying to cling to a rock by the riverside won't help. And, most of the time this is what we are attempting to do. Total surrendering to the river of life, and moving with it towards the destination it will take us seem too scary because there is the thrill of the unknown. We rather prefer the false security of the stagnant water by the river side to the vibrant river moving with a splendid energy. We will begin to live fully only when we surrender totally to the river, and begin moving with it towards the vast ocean, because the very meaning of life is hidden in the river joining the ocean.

Practical suggestions on moving with the river of life:
-Accept the facts of your life as they are without having inner resistance. Do what you can to change things in your life if you wish to, but do not resist inwardly, because that very resistance is like

trying to walk against the current of a powerful river which will damage you. Just move with the river effortlessly.

-Live dangerously with an adventurous spirit.

-Stop seeking security inwardly as psychological security is an impossible illusion. Your life will be wasted if you try to reach this impossibility. Just secure the physical body, and that is enough.

Letter#35
February 05, 2013

"When one goes to a party of the neighbor for a night, one simply enjoys as a guest without the conflict and complications of being attached. As time is relative, this 'one night' can be extended to 'one life', and one can live this 'one life' as a guest on earth."

The Guest House

What would happen if we falsely think we own a house in which we are just a temporary guest for some time? First of all, we would be in total illusion away from the fact that we are just a guest in this house. Secondly, there would be perpetual conflict between the fact of us being only a temporary guest and our illusion of owning the house.

The absolute fact is we are guests in this marvellous world for some temporary period of time which might be 70, 80, 90 or hundred years. As time is a relative thing, our lives are not really long especially if we do not live it in the great depths of silence where time slows down. But we are guests, and this is the absolute and irrevocable fact. Human problem starts when this fact is resisted by escaping the peaceful acceptance of the fact of death. Can we accept the fact that we are guests on this earth, and live accordingly? The implications of this acceptance which are same like staying in a guest house are as below:

-Not getting attached to the things of the guest house like the furniture in it as you know you will have to leave them. In the same way, can we live our lives without being attached to our houses, cars, bank accounts… etc?

-We are naturally ready to leave the guest house anytime without taking roots there. Can we live without taking deep roots of any kind anywhere so that we are always free to move?
-We accept the fact of temporary stay in the guest house without conflict, and enjoy this temporary time. Can we also accept the fact of temporary stay in this world without conflict, thus enjoy our remaining time, and leave peacefully when the time comes?

If we go to a guest house, and instead of enjoying the temporary stay as a guest, we want to own and take roots in that place to be permanent, then naturally there would be eternal conflict simply because what we are attempting to do is an impossible thing. The feeling of owning nothing inwardly will make one so light spiritually, and that is what is needed. One might own a house or a bank account on the paper, but can one own nothing inwardly? This means, the 'me' who says 'I own a big house' should stop owning things within the skin. Then, Intelligence will be there as a quality of awareness to physically own things such as a house, but no feeling of the 'me' owning a house will be there. Simply, one will own things out there in the physical world, but not within the mind as the 'I' possessing those things. This feeling of possession of things in the mind is to be eradicated. Only then, we can live as a guest in this world, and to go deeper into oneself to see the 'me' in the process of owning and possessing things in many different subtle ways is part of meditation. Why do we have this craving to possess things? Why can't we have things like a car or a wife without any seeking of possession on them?

Life will be a paradise if we live as we are in 'the guest house', and a place of eternal conflict in the 'my house'. Leaving the 'my house' and moving to the 'guest house' as a way of living will make one feel very light and free spiritually, and joy can only visit the guest house but never the 'my house' which has the feeling of a prison because of the limitations involved; whereas there is the splendid scent of freedom spread in the air of the 'guest house'.

When one goes to a party of the neighbor for a night, one simply enjoys as a guest without the conflict and complications of being attached. As time is relative, this 'one night' can be extended to 'one life', and one can live this 'one life' as a guest on this lovely earth.

Practical suggestions on 'The Guest House':
-Live in this world as a guest who is ready to depart anytime; thus do not take strong roots.
-Always be prepared spiritually for death which means no attachment of any kind.
-Meditate upon the fundamental difference between living in this world as a guest and as an owner.

Letter#36
February 14, 2013

"To be truly spiritual, one must have the rationality of an excellent scientist, and the tender heart of a mother who just gave birth to a new life."

Rational Spirituality

Spirituality which is not rational in its relationship to one's daily life is not spirituality at all. It is merely an abstraction in a dream world which has very little meaning. There must be no element in spirituality which is non-factual. Simple logic and reasoning with its intelligence must be an important part of such spiritual attitude. Without such intelligence, so called spirituality means very little. Rationality, reasoning and intelligence are the most important tools to be used on the spiritual path. Spirituality is not about following a guru or methods of meditation. Spirituality is about climbing the mountain of truth which can only be done by questioning everything with rational intelligence, and discarding that which is false consequently. The guru, with his methods of living, is a heavy weight which must be thrown away in this climb. The only tool that one can rely on in this journey to the top is one's own rational questioning.

In such rational spirituality, one will move from one fact to another in daily life. Those who escape from the realities of life into a secluded so called spiritual withdrawal are merely deceiving themselves with an illusion of spirituality. They simply do not want to face the facts of life. What does it mean to move from one fact to another? It is simple seeing of the facts of life and moving accordingly. For instance, the very first fact of life is that one must make a living for proper food, clothes and shelter. The next fact is about what kind of job one will love to do. This might demand deep questioning to find out what one really loves to do. Saying, "One cannot be spiritual in this corrupt business life" is the denial of intelligent rationality; hence it is also the denial of spirituality. One must, and one will find a rational way of doing business or making a living without being part of the corruption of today's society. Such spirituality with its intelligence will also be a part of one's business life. There is absolutely a rational way of living in relationship with society, and without such relationship one cannot be spiritual; but one will become more and more isolated. So spirituality, rationality, questioning, reasoning and intelligence are an inseparable whole. Any form of so called spirituality without all these other elements included is nothing but a form of isolation from the reality of life into an illusory way of living. Intelligence must function in the truly spiritual person's daily life in order to deal with life rationally.

To be truly spiritual, one must have the rationality of an excellent scientist and the tender heart of a mother who just gave birth to a new life. Love intrinsically contains such rationality and intelligence within itself. There is no such a thing as love without rational intelligence. Love has nothing to do with romantic illusions. Now, there might be a certain sense of rationality, questioning and reasoning among the materialist philosophers and thinkers, but they are not spiritual as they themselves declare. So, what is the difference between rational spirituality and rational thinking? There are quite many different factors which must be involved to answer this question, but to put it very very simply, we can say;
rational thinking+love and compassion=rational spirituality

In the future, there might be computers or robots with extraordinary rationality and artificial intelligence, but no type of intelligence can come close to the natural intelligence of love.

Practical suggestions on rational spirituality:
-Always remember that if your spirituality does not include rational intelligence in its relationship with simple everyday living, then it is

not spirituality at all. It is merely a form of escape from the facts of life.

-Be a pragmatic who is living with the facts all the time rather than being a spiritual dreamer who is away from the facts.

-Always make sure you have love and compassion in your heart on top of your pragmatism; otherwise you will become a pragmatic only with a frozen heart.

-When you hear a sincere voice saying, "I do not agree"; listen attentively because that might be truth speaking to you as a signpost showing the right path. Be extremely awake and willing to listen to sincere critics rather than listening to empty flatteries. While such sincere critics hold the great power to awaken you spiritually, empty flatteries are equally powerful to put you in a deep state of sleep. Critical awareness is the path of spiritual awakening.

Letter#37
February 26, 2013

"Just leave everything inwardly. This is what death means; leaving everything we hold on to firmly. Joy is to be found only in such ending of the 'me'. In that ending, there is rejuvenation. Only in ending, there is a new beginning."

Making peace with death

Wouldn't it be a better life if we make peace with the worst enemy? As it is now, our worst enemy in living is death. There is immediate terror in our minds even only by hearing the word itself. Why? Why can we not accept this irrevocable fact of life totally with peace? Why is ending such a scary thing? And, what changes if we make a final peace with death?

Death is probably the greatest fear of mankind among many other fears. It might be called as the mother of all fears, and when that mother dies she can't give birth to new fears. Wouldn't making total peace with death imply the ending of the fear of death; thus the ending of all fear? After all, if one is really free from the fear of death totally, then what more is there to fear from? And, one can live with joy only when one is free from all fear. If this is so, how can we make peace with death?

What does death mean? Doesn't it mean ending? What ends? The physical body, and the 'me' or the 'ego' with all the memories of a life long time come to an end. What is important here is the ending of the 'me', because we wouldn't fear death if we are given a more beautiful physical body to have a next life with the same 'me' in it. But, a new body with another 'me' does not mean much. So, what is really important for us, and what we really dread most is the ending of the 'me' only. The ending of the physical body is a secondary issue in the fear of death. If this is so, then making peace with death simply means making peace with the concept of ending of the 'me'. What then would the ending of the 'me' mean? To put it very very simple, it means the ending of any sense of continuity. This includes our attachments, pleasures, desire to be rich and successful etc. Basically, it is the ending of all the factors which make up the 'me'. Can all that come to an end totally? If that is possible, then we will meet death while the body is alive, therefore we will be free from the fear of death and all other fears of any kind as a natural consequence. One can possibly ask whether it would be a life of vegetation if there is such an ending in the psyche. This must be discovered by oneself only by delving deep into this question of ending. After all, if we do not like that state of the mind, we can always come back to our current state which is nothing but confusion and suffering. So, nothing could be worse really. But, if one goes far enough to that depth, then one will see that in such psychological ending there is great joy and fresh ecstatic energy of life. In fact, joy is to be found only in such ending of the 'me'. In that ending, there is rejuvenation. Only in ending, there is a new beginning. Continuity is decay.

In the moment of such total psychological ending, the body and the psyche will be energized immediately. In fact, even a split of a second of such ending in a day will bring such magnitude of energy that will be more than enough to have a completely happy day. This is like letting go off everything inwardly, and a sense of total surrender which will remove the psychological burden of the endless chattering and the continuity of the 'me'. It is a kind of a feeling and a state of a mind in which you do not mind anything even if you hear on the news that the world will end that day. Basically, the 'me' is leaving everything it is holding on to. Do it sometimes when you are alone and see the energy flow. When you try, you will realize how difficult it is for us to leave this world totally even for a second. To leave the husband, the wife, the children, the house, the car, the bank account etc. Again, this does not mean a kind of vegetation. On the contrary, if you can psychologically end this way, then with the quality of heightened mental energy, you will have quite a different kind of totally vital relationship with life and with your loved ones as well. You will touch the supreme energy only by such ending, and then you can enjoy life like never before.

Just leave everything inwardly. This is what death means; leaving everything we hold on to firmly. If we can live this way, then living and dying becomes one, and death then is not something to be feared at the end of our lives. This is what it means to make peace with death, and only in making peace with death, one will find true peace in life. After all, there has been billions who lived and died on this earth, and many more billions are there yet to come, live and die. You are just one out of these billions who will inevitably experience death. So, you are not alone.

How complicated existence becomes when our petty little 'self' imagines itself as the most important thing of this vast universe. The fact is that the 'self' will, sooner or later, have to join those billions who also once thought of themselves as the most important thing. Death is the irrevocable fact of life. Why not simply accept this fact peacefully rather than living in an eternal battle of an impossible resistance to it. Wouldn't it be wiser and happier to live in peace with death rather than being at war with it all one's life? And, the only way to have an absolute sense of peace with death is to enter into the house of death while living by ending the 'me'. The choice is yours. The wise will take the peaceful path of inward acceptance of this absolute fact of life; and the otherwise will live in eternal conflict by resisting it. Just die to the 'me' and live happily in the rest of your days on this earth free from the fear of death instead of wasting them in fear. So, you have two choices and not three for the rest of your life; first is to live free from the fear of death, and second is to live in that terrible darkness of fear. And, you will have to live those days anyway whether you like it or not; so wouldn't it be simply wiser to live without fear? Living with fear won't prevent death anyway, so why not live without it happily? It seems very reasonable to drop fear immediately if we look at it from this point of view, but we can't. What is preventing us then to drop fear **now** without the complications of time being involved? If we can't drop fear today, then no tomorrow will be the cure. Going deep into the question of ending fear this way is part of meditation.

Practical suggestions on making peace with death:
-Be aware of all kinds of obvious and subtle desires of the mind for inward continuity.
-Be aware of the deeply rooted fear of death in the consciousness, and meditate upon this fear to bridge the gap between life and death. Life cannot be without death. These two make up an inseparable whole. See the truth of this, and live your life with the light of this truth.
-Jump off an imaginary inward psychological cliff sometimes, and die inwardly to everything which means ending all attachment; and incarnate in the now again. In such ending, there is joyful rejuvenation.
- Whether you are ready or not, someday it will all come to an end. There will be no more sunrises, no minutes, hours or days. All the things you collected, whether treasured or forgotten will pass to someone else. Your wealth, fame and power will be irrelevant. It will not matter what you owned or what you were owed. Your grudges, resentments, frustrations and jealousies will finally disappear. So too, your hopes, ambitions, plans and your do lists will expire. The wins and losses that mattered so much for you will fade away. It won't matter where you came from or what side of the tracks you lived on. It won't matter whether you were beautiful or brilliant. Even your gender and skin color will be irrelevant. What will matter though is whether you lived with the light of joy and true love. Remembering death sometimes, not as a morbid subject, but as an irrevocable fact of life, will help us to keep rooted in the present moment by reminding us nothing is permanent, and no future is guaranteed. Then, enjoyment in the deepening awareness of the present moment becomes the most important thing, and this strong connection with

the present through the fact of death will naturally bring a quality of love and joy into our lives.

- If you are told by a doctor 'actually, not theoretically', that you have got exactly 1 year left to live, how would you change your life? Wouldn't you love more? Or, for example, would you be as busy, as angry, as stressful, as hating, as ambitious, as bored, as depressed as you are now? Can you find out what would change in your life with a realistic scenario of having only a year left to live, and can you start applying those changes to your life now? Ask this question **seriously** like it is true and meditate upon it in silence, as the answer has great genuine potential to change your life radically in a positive direction.

Letter#38
March 10, 2013

"Imagine the way this ancient commune of hundred that discovered truth and love would live. Wouldn't the very way of their living naturally be spiritual? They would all love one another selflessly. They would help one another whenever needed. They would share the things they have willingly and happily simply because they love each other. They would simply be like a family of sisters and brothers. The secret key of this commune would be 'selflessness', as they would have discovered the absolute fact that love and selfishness cannot coexist."

Birth of Spirituality
When and why did ancient humanity demand spirituality? What is the origin of it? When did it all begin?

Let's take a journey back to the very ancient times when humanity first began. To make it very very simple, try to imagine yourself as a member of the commune of the first hundred human beings on earth. You found yourself on planet earth knowing absolutely nothing about anything. You have already seen the death of some members of the commune, and you understood they left permanently, and one day you too will have to leave too; but at the same time the survival instinct in you is naturally fighting to find food. You are basically in the middle of an unknown chaos both inwardly and outwardly, and out of this great uncertainty the first drop of fear has fallen into your mind, and that is where the demand and the need for spirituality, god or a creator who will somehow give you a feeling of mental security came into being. So, out of fear, ancient spirituality has begun. As fear is darkness, such form of spirituality whose origin is in darkness, or which came into being as a reaction to darkness of fear naturally cannot lead to light. Light has absolutely no relationship with darkness, and this includes the opposites type of relationship as well. Each opposite has its roots in its own opposite, and without one the other cannot exist by itself. But, is light the opposite of darkness, or does light exist alone by itself?

Apart from such type of spirituality which was born out of fear, and which continued until today; were there other human beings at the very beginning of humankind who lived differently in a way which was naturally spiritual? Let's imagine then another commune of hundred at the very beginnings of life on earth whose members have discovered for themselves the beauty of loving one another by questioning everything to find out the truth of life for themselves instead of going for the easy way of believing in an idea of god that was born out of fear and uncertainty .They had to discover such truth and love by themselves because fortunately or unfortunately there were no saviors, no gurus, no Jesus, no Buddha then to instruct them. So, they had to find out for themselves the truth of life simply because they had no other choice. So, think of yourself as one of these ancient human beings, and ask yourself the question, "What would I do without Jesus, the Buddha or my petty little guru etc."? And, once this question is put honestly to oneself, the truth of spirituality will come into being naturally; which is, there is no need for any savior or guru to be spiritual. On the contrary, acceptance of any authority in one's inner journey becomes the greatest hindrance in the spiritual search. Such ancient people had to do their inward job by themselves by putting their teeth into this thing to find out, because fortunately there was probably no guru business then. And, this is the only way to be truly spiritual. There is no other way. One must start one's spiritual path like the first human being who knows nothing about any form of spirituality, and walk from there to discover for oneself. After all, no book or no guru can teach what love is. Love is something we have to discover for ourselves. And, without love, there is no spirituality.

Imagine the way this ancient commune of hundred that discovered truth and love would live. Wouldn't the very way of their living naturally be spiritual? They would all love one another selflessly. They would help one another whenever needed. They would share the things they have willingly and happily simply because they love each other, and not because some guru or a so called holy book has told to do so. They would never compare themselves with another inwardly; as such comparison is the greatest enemy of love. They would simply be like a family of sisters and brothers. The secret key of this commune would be 'selflessness' since they would have discovered the absolute fact that love and selfishness cannot coexist. This commune would be terribly spiritual. One could feel the true spirituality in the air the moment one goes into this commune. And, the irony would be that they would be truly and naturally spiritual simply because they had this quality of love, whereas modern humanity with its millions of books about spirituality simply does not love, thus they are just playing with some false ideas of spirituality as a form of entertainment. In this commune, there would be no divisions as the skin color, nationality, religion, the beautiful and the ugly etc. There would be no spiritual levels either like those who claim they attained Nirvana, god, bliss.. etc. as love knows no such different levels among human beings. They would simply be a commune living in the natural harmony of love; therefore they would be naturally spiritual without even consciously knowing they are spiritual which, in fact, is the only way of being truly spiritual. Love truly, and you will be spiritual. For such love to come into being, one must understand the extremely subtle ways of the 'self' or the 'ego', and through such understanding and awareness, freedom from the 'self' will perhaps bring about this quality of love.

One might think, as many probably will, that such way of living is nothing but an unattainable utopia. This inherently brings the question of whether true love is a utopia or not. Only those who are not willing to love will see it as a utopia. One might also think what difference would it make if one loves when almost all the world is lacking this quality of love. This is the good old lazy trick. The answer to this is, "Let me love first and see what happens." And, there have been rare individuals in the history of mankind who said so, and they made great difference by effecting human consciousness. If one individual radically changes his or her way of living , then that change will naturally have its effects on the world.

Practical suggestions on spirituality:

-Understand love is the essence of a spiritual life, and without love there is no spirituality, but do not try to find the way to love. There is no such a thing as how to love. Love must find its own way naturally like the love of a mother for her baby. Love can not be learned from books or others, and you can not go towards it, because it has no particular path. Just be aware of what love is not, and such awareness itself will become the waves of love. See love is not jealousy, hatred, selfishness or comparing ourselves with the others.

-Understand that love and selfishness can not go together, and just be aware of selfishness with all its subtlety in your relationships with others. Do not try to be unselfish in order to be good, spiritual or loving, because trying to be unselfish in order to be good is still the activity of selfishness at a more subtle level in a different direction. True goodness which has no selfishness in it must flower naturally because of seeing the danger of selfishness. Trying to build a good personality is just another very tricky game of selfishness. What is important is seeing and ending selfishness completely in any direction rather than building up an unselfish personality which really has no meaning.

-Never accept the authority of another in the spiritual area. Listen to what others are saying because wisdom implies one must have a state of mind which says "I do not know" so that one is able to listen. Only then one can truly learn. Listen, but find out for yourself the truth or the falseness of what is being said.

-Be aware that love is the secret doctrine which by itself will easily bring perfect order, balance and happiness to our lives.

Letter#39
March 21, 2013

"Love looked at the extraordinary beauty of the splendid full moon for a few minutes before she left the lovely earth, and she thought human beings must ask a fundamental question as they were all waiting for love and happiness to knock on their door. And, the question in her mind that must be asked by each human being was; 'If I were the eternal love and the sacred compassion, would I knock on my door?' "

Love takes a journey to the world

One day love decided to take a journey to the world for a day to enjoy the beautiful earth, and stay over for a night as a guest in a house to spend some time with humans whom she loved so much. After seeing some of the most beautiful scenes of the earth, she began walking down the streets of the world to find a door to knock on in order to be the guest for the night. Along with her, she carried some presents from heavens to be given to the people who will have her as a guest for the night.

She started from the Religious Street where the believers of the organized religions lived. She was so extraordinarily sensitive that she could feel the atmosphere of the street just by seeing some people walking around. She sensed the feeling of restrictions, rules and lack of freedom. Their religions were so little, so petty, so static in beliefs and limited that it was literally impossible for the limitless dynamic quality of love with its freedom to find its way to this religious street. She looked around at people, she observed and she said to herself, "I am love, I am free, I am bound to tell the truth. These people seem to be quite unhappy, and if I tell these people the truth that what they believe is false and they can never find true happiness, peace and love in such beliefs, then they would get offended. So, this street is not a good one for me to spend my only night in the world. I want to find a house where really happy people live so that we can all have some great time."

She continued walking, and all of a sudden she entered the Spiritual Street. This street was quite more interesting compared to the religious one. People looked more balanced, more free and more peaceful. She observed the people of the street very carefully again and she saw, though they do not have a belief of god as somebody sitting up in the sky, they had certain strange rituals, certain methods, certain practices, certain gurus which in a subtle way replaced the belief in god of the religious street. They were quite lost in the so called spirituality that they seemed to forget the most essential thing of spirituality which is love, happiness and compassion that have nothing to do with any kind of methods, rituals or gurus. They were all talking about love, bliss and compassion; but they were in love with their spiritual rituals, methods or gurus instead of falling in love with life itself which is only true guru. They were like people who were endlessly talking about the methods of how to get out of the prison when they stand just next to the prison door, and the only thing they needed to do was to simply open the door and walk out. But for them, talking about how to open the door with its different methods was much more important than the simple act of opening the door. After such observation love said to herself, "I am love, I am free, I am bound to tell the truth, and if I tell them the truth that their rituals, methods and gurus are absolutely meaningless, and they rather become a heavy burden to carry on the path of climbing the mountain of truth and happiness, then they would get terribly offended. So, this is not the right place for me either."

She was beginning to get a little bit disappointed when she walked in to the Atheist Street. She sensed something different immediately on this street. Though the people looked very honest and intelligent, they seemed to suffer much more than the people of the other two streets she has visited. At least, she felt she could have the freedom to tell the truth here without being offended much, but it wouldn't be a happy night either as there was a strong sense of suffering in the air; the kind of suffering of the human beings who had the futile attempt of denying the undeniable spiritual side of a human being as human beings are spiritual creatures by nature. She did not know what to do. She said to herself, "It seems there is no perfect place I can find to spend the night as a guest, but I love human beings so much, and I want to spend some time with them. I am getting quite tired, and maybe there is a reason why this street was the last to be visited." And, she walked towards the house next to her to knock on the door when she heard the shouting coming from the house; it was probably a man yelling at his wife; "We don't believe in stupid things like the divine love on this street, but at least we could have full respect for one another to be able to live under the same roof in a logic relationship." This was probably a sign to show love that it would be a better idea to leave the world, and spend the night in heavens.

It was exactly at that time when she decided to leave the world that she heard a voice calling for her. She said to herself, "This is what I love about life on earth. Good things happen when there is no more hope left, no more seeking anymore, and generally on the last minute. Life takes you to the best places in the journey only through this beautiful thrilling path of adventure. What a beautiful thing this living is! I wonder what god do these humans worship or seek when there is life itself there to be worshipped."

"What are you looking for?" the voice said. It was a man around his early sixties. "I am love. I took a journey to the world for a day, and I am looking for a place to be a guest for tonight." love replied the man. The man looked at her quite puzzled; he took some time before he spoke. There was a certain quality of wisdom in his eyes, and he said, "You are lucky to see me here at this time of the night. There is only one place I can suggest you as only they can understand somebody like you who calls herself love coming from heavens. People think they are strange, since they are totally different people in their way of living as they do not give much importance to the material things of the world, but in fact they are quite nice people. They live on the Truth Seekers Street."

Love immediately felt the real difference of the Truth Seekers Street soon after she entered. "Finally!", she said to herself, "I found the right place thanks to that poor chap. I now understand why I went to the Atheist Street lastly. I was meant to meet that man in order to come here." The people whom she observed on the street looked very sincere, healthy and vital. These people were very open minded in their spiritual search. They had no static beliefs, rituals or methods since they seem to have grasped a simple fact that truth which is life itself is a dynamic and living thing; therefore it cannot be approached by any static means which are all those so called spiritual methods, rituals or beliefs. Therefore, they seemed to have the quality of the freedom in the mind to listen to the new. They haven't got stuck with any of those static means, thus they had the quality of the swiftness of the mind which can seek the dynamic living truth. Love felt very comfortable on this street as she felt totally free here to say all the truth she knew. Nobody would oppose hearing the truth here; after all, truth was what they were seeking for anyway. And, she could spend a happy night with them as they were quite happy, good hearted and sincere people.

Love started walking down the street to find a house to knock its door to be a guest for that night. She approached the door of one house, but as she approached the house she smelled some blood in the air. Love was extremely sensitive with her senses, and she got the smell of the blood of the beef which was being prepared for dinner in that house. Feeling the smell of the blood, love said to herself; "I am love, I am compassion, how can I be a guest to a house where there is the smell of fresh blood in the air. A life which is sacred to me has just been murdered in this house. I know these people do not see it this way; and they are indeed very very nice people with truly good hearts, but I am too very sensitive to be a guest in a house where there is the smell of fresh blood in the air."

Love turned her back, and said to herself; "People all around the world are seeking happiness and love. They do all kinds of things for me to knock on their door so that their suffering souls are transformed by my touch, and I have done my best to knock on the door to be with them, to touch them, to heal them as my love for them is eternal; but only the extremely few seem to prepare their houses well enough for me to be able knock on the door."

Love looked at the extraordinary beauty of the splendid full moon for a few minutes before she left the lovely earth, and she thought human beings must ask a fundamental question as they were all waiting for love and happiness to knock on their door. And, the question in her mind that must be asked by each human being was; 'If I were the eternal love and the sacred compassion, would I knock on my door?'

Letter#40
March 31, 2013

The real question which is also the ultimate and only solution to this problem of sex is; "Can man and woman selflessly love one another without seeking any personal pleasure so that every time they touch one another, it is like the first time in which they feel a natural ecstasy just like the very first man and woman on this earth discovering that very original touch in the garden of joy?"

The original touch

How did the very first touch come? It must be instinctive, because it cannot be a learned one since it is the very first touch. Imagine yourself for a moment, as the first man or woman on earth. All of a sudden you see the opposite sex, of course naked. The very seeing of the opposite sex naked would not arise any sexual feelings, because there is no memory of sex yet. Then, you just look at the opposite sex with great astonishment, rather than with any sexual temptations. Basically, it is seeing something totally new which you have no recorded memory of. Then, you just look and want to discover that thing. At the same time, there was probably a strong instinctive force of attraction which is planted in humans by nature, and this perhaps started to pull the opposite sexes to one another sexually. This force of attraction must have been there for human race to continue.

Then, the two sexes got closer by physical distance naturally to discover more about the opposite sex, and the closer they got physically, the force of attraction began to pull them towards one another much stronger like two magnets coming closer; perhaps with an irresistible magnitude. And, the man probably had the first touch, and there it all began.

Both the man and the woman have sensed something different in this first touch. A great sense of joy, and a great uncontrollable desire to touch more, and it was not something they were doing by thinking, but it was that immensely strong whirlwind for unity or oneness which is in operation, and basically it was impossible to resist it. There was no reason to resist it anyway because it was mankind's destiny to reproduce on this earth, and there was nothing wrong in this first experience of sexuality as it was a natural part of the living process. This very first touch was pure and innocent because it was all about a joyful discovery of a splendid fruit of living, and not seeking of pleasure, because seeking of pleasure can only take place when there is a recorded memory of the experience that is being sought.

Then, what happened? Why did sexuality lose that original beauty of the very first touch? Then, thought took the memory of the beauty of that original touch, and desired to have it again more and more which turned it into the pleasure seeking process; hence the vicious cycle of sexual problem had begun. It has been a problem, because pleasure seeking is inseparable from pain. Pleasure and pain are the two inseparable sides of one coin. The very seeking of any pleasure is time bounded, as one can seek only what is recorded in the memory as a past experience of pleasure. This very seeking itself implies attachment to the pleasure that is being sought, and the formation of the attachment bond inevitably and inherently brings pain within itself.

Then, human beings had this new problem of sexuality as a baby in their hands. Not knowing how to deal with it intelligently, religions restricted it brutally, but this was going against the dynamics of the nature itself; therefore this attitude added to the problem making it worse than before. Then came a new era as a reaction to the restrictions of religions, and they suggested total freedom and indulging in sexuality. The freedom part was ok, at least better than the restrictive approach of the religions, but mere indulging in sexuality as it is the only and the most important thing in life has not been an answer to the problem itself. It simply strengthened the attachment bond of sexual pleasure which again made the problem into a complex one in another direction.

Finally, we have come to the modern times of today, and sexuality is basically an ordinary pleasure like the football match now. Humanity is so ignorantly lost in indulging in it. It has totally lost the innocent beauty and the joy of the very first touch. There was no sin in the very first touch. That very first touch was a beautiful part of the celebration of living, but it was a part, and not the whole. Unfortunately, today it became the most important thing of people's lives, and the total celebration of the beauty of living has died long time ago. Sexuality, as it is now in today's world, has very little meaning if not none.

So, it was thought, the self or the ego which started its operations by seeking the pleasure of the very first touch, therefore it destroyed the original quality and beauty. There was no sense of self or ego, no seeking of personal sensual pleasure in that original touch which made it an innocent one. So, there is nothing wrong in the sexual act itself as long as it is has the quality of pure selfless innocence which can only come when there is real love between man and woman. It seems this quality of real love is missing in these modern times. So there is nothing right, wrong or sinful in sexuality itself, as with drinking water since it is a natural part of living, but it has become a problem when the self or the ego started playing with it. The same self, not knowing how to deal with it intelligently, condemned it by calling it a sin, tortured itself with brutal restrictions, then again the self decided to indulge in it, but the problem is still there with an ever increasing momentum of conflict, and human beings still seem to be so very ignorant in the ways they deal with this problem.

The real question which is also the ultimate and only solution to this problem of sex is; "Can man and woman selflessly love one another without seeking any personal pleasure so that every time they touch one another, it is like the first time in which they feel a natural ecstasy just like the very first man and woman on this earth discovering that very original touch in the garden of joy?"

Letter#41
April 11, 2013

"Elimination of fear and inward conflicts will naturally bring about the true sense of peace; just like the sun coming out when the clouds are gone. Think of a moment of your life when you really loved, when you had a true feeling in your heart for another, for the tree or for a cat; at that very moment there was no fear and no conflict because the light of love wiped away all darkness, and the sun came into being. That sun is love, peace and joy, and they all go together."

Peace

What is peace? Not the so called peace in between two wars of nations, but peace inwardly. Obviously, as it is now, the world is not a peaceful place at all, and since the world is a mere reflection of the individual, it seems human beings are not in peace psychologically. This is a blatant fact of the world today. Humanity is craving for some inner peace. And not finding it, they become destructive both for their own lives, and for the life of the planet we share.

What does it mean to be peaceful inwardly? Can one be peaceful when one is in conflict of any kind? What is the factor which can bring this true sense of peace to our lives? To find out, we perhaps have to look for the origin of the chaos within ourselves. Why are we restless all the time? Why can't we simply enjoy this beautiful gift of living? Obviously, something is preventing us. What is that something which prevents peace coming into our lives?

Can there be peace when one has psychological fears of any kind? This is a very simple question, and the answer is within the question itself. Obviously not! There cannot possibly be this absolute sense of peace when one is burdened with the darkness of fear. So, psychological fear of any kind is one of the major factors which prevent peace coming into our lives. Having seen this as a fact, what is the proper way of dealing with fear? Can any religious beliefs, worshipping, prayer or so called meditation technique free the mind from fear? Or, fear is there for us to look, observe study and understand so that the mind is freed from fear at the very origin? How can belief in god or any other belief free the mind from fear? My belief in god or belief of any kind is basically an idea I have because of the laziness of the mind to think out and find out the truth of things for itself. It's been thousands of years since human beings began on this earth, and they have had thousands of gods, so called spiritual rituals, meditation methods, religions; and none has freed human beings from fear, and unless one frees oneself from psychological fear totally, one will never know the light of true peace. Such freedom can only come through observation and the understanding such observation brings about. When one has a problem with the engine of one's car what does one do? One looks at the problem to find the very origin of the problem. No belief will help, nor any technique. One must look and identify the problem at the very origin. In the same way, can we look at fear in the very depths of our consciousness? The very fear of looking at fear itself and chasing it until its very origin is already the first obstacle to be eliminated to begin with.

Can there be peace when one is in inward conflict of any kind? If I compare myself with another inwardly, can I ever find peace? Say for instance, if I compare my success, my physical appearance, my wealth, my so called spirituality...etc. with another, then does not this kind of comparison imply perpetual conflict? If so, can I live without any sense of inward comparison of myself with another? What is the need of such comparison anyway? We can compare things in the physical world, but what meaning does the psychological comparison of oneself with another have other than bringing conflict to one's life? Then, one must realize that such comparison is another factor which prevents peace coming into our lives with its beauty and full effect, and with such realization one must end all such inward comparison immediately today, and not tomorrow, because if time comes in then action in the now which is the only solution to any problem will be blocked.

Can desire also be another source of conflict? What is wrong with desire at the actual moment of perception of a beautiful thing? What is wrong in desiring a nice dress one sees in a shop? Nothing! We are living things, and desire is a normal, healthy thing as long as it does not have continuity in time. I see the dress, I like it and desire arises. There is nothing wrong until this point, but the problem and conflict begins when I think about the dress, imagine myself in the dress...etc. Can I simply have the desire at the moment of perception, and then die to that desire the next moment totally, so that I live in the present moment all the time with what I am doing. If I have the money tomorrow, then I will go and buy that dress; and if I don't, then I won't. This demands great sense of inward simplicity with its supreme intelligence. If I have money I will, if I do not I won't. What is important is health and being happy with life itself first with a healthy body. Where is then conflict of desire in this kind of approach? There is none. Conflict arises only if that desire has its continuity, and then it becomes the play thing of the self, the ego.

This is part of true meditation. Finding out whether it is possible to live with desire which is a natural and healthy thing without letting it creating inner conflict is the true art of meditation. If one totally lives in the present moment, then I see the dress, have a desire for it, and then the next minute I totally die to the memory of the dress while I am enjoying my afternoon tea with full attention in the new present moment I enter into; but if my attention is divided with the memory of the dress I have seen, then my new present moment of enjoying the tea will be wasted. In that case, neither the tea nor the dress can make me happy because I fall into the conflict of moving away from the present moment which is created by desire as a result of the lack of awareness of the movement of desire. So, desire must not be suppressed or destroyed, but it is to be understood.

So, elimination of fear and inward conflicts will naturally bring about the true sense of peace, just like the sun coming out when the clouds are gone. Think of a moment of your life when you really loved, when you had a true feeling in your heart for another, for the tree or for a cat; at that very moment there was no fear and no conflict, as the light of love wiped away all darkness, and the sun came into being. That sun is love, peace and joy, and they all go together.

Practical suggestions on peace:
-Do natural yoga exercises such as hiking and swimming as much as possible.
-Do not compare yourself with another inwardly.
-Sit quietly sometimes, and just watch the things passing by around you without any judgments or a word. Watch the bird in its flight, or watch the river flowing by. Just, silently watch.
-Have a vegetarian diet as much as possible.
-Try to be away from people and environments where you feel lack of love.
- Spending time in nature has a great healing effect both physically and psychologically as well. It is good to go for a hike in nature as much as possible for instance. One must also be alone sometimes in nature for better communication with nature and for better healing effects. You will hear the joyful singing of mother nature better when you spend some time alone in her compassionate hands. If somehow one does not have much time, or one feels lazy for a hike, then even

watching the green of nature has healing and silencing effect on the mind. Watch nature silently as much as possible. Even 10 minutes each day if possible will make a lot of difference for the mind to become silent and peaceful. Just watch quietly.

- If the electricity is cut off in your area for about 2 hours at night, you will naturally have to be away from facebook, internet, TV etc. And, if you are lucky enough to have a candle, you will spend this period with your loved ones, or alone under the candle light. Would your mind be more in a state of silent meditative peace in this period, and why if it would?

Letter#42
April 26, 2013

"So, try to experience life as a silent camera recording, of course, with the vibrant living quality of awareness which a camera can never have. But, a camera can never judge what is being recorded. In the same way, sometimes when you are with friends, just be like this silent camera for a few minutes just witnessing what is taking place, and see what happens. You will realize then, it is this deep sense of silence beyond, which is in operation through you rather than the 'self', or the 'ego'. That silence is true peace."

Observation

The wise have all said that the key to joyful wisdom lies in knowing oneself, and to know oneself, one must observe for sure. To learn about anything we must observe that thing closely and quietly, mustn't we? And, can we learn about the thing we observe if any judgment interferes with the observation? Let's say I am observing a friend, and the moment I say, "How stupid or how intelligent she is"; at that very moment objective and intelligent observation which is true learning comes to an end. So, can we observe without any interference of thought? Thought is the noisy sound in the mind, and when there is no such sound, then there is the silent observation which will take us to the path of learning and wisdom.

How does a video camera record? It just records silently without any judgment of what is being recorded, but at the same time there is no consciousness or intelligent awareness of what is being recorded. Compared to human mind, a camera is a dead machine. Now, a human mind is looking around and recording just like a camera, but of course because there is a living quality of the mind; other things interfere in this recording as well. As it is now, the talking mind with its judgments always interfere with such recording. For instance, human mind might say, "What a beautiful car" during the process of such recording. So, basically we have an inbuilt camera which is on all the time except the sleeping hours. A camera just records silently. There is no quality of intelligent observation and awareness. Now, when the noisy sound of thought and ego ends in human mind, then human mind automatically becomes like this camera with life added to it, and that quality of life is awareness and intelligent observation. There is no conflict in such functioning of the mind. Conflict begins the moment thought or the ego comes into being. So, try sometimes to experience life as a silent camera recording without a center as the 'I'; of course with a vitally living quality of awareness which a camera can never have, but a camera can never judge what is being recorded as well. In the same way, sometimes when you are with friends, just be like this silent camera for a few minutes just witnessing what is taking place, and see what happens. You will realize then, it is this deep sense of silence beyond which is in operation through you rather than the 'self', or the 'ego'. That silence is true peace.

Then, take this record from the camera and watch like you are watching a movie. How do you watch a movie? You do not say, "Let me change this or that", but you just watch it. Can we watch ourselves like we are watching a character in a movie? We cannot change certain qualities like jealousy, anger, loneliness...etc. of this character in this movie, but we can watch and be aware. Can we silently watch ourselves this way with no attempt whatsoever to change "what is" which is basically ourselves? Just silent recording and watching with no judgments or any kind of sound of the mind. Such process will slow down the movement of thought and ego with its everlasting chattering, and will bring stillness to the mind at great depths. Wisdom is this very process of silent observation which will go deeper and deeper by itself once it starts.

Practical suggestions on observation:
-Observe with no judgments or words. Just look without a word. Don't say good or bad, but just watch.
-Let the silence observe through you rather than "you" as the observer taking place in the observation. For this silence to come into being, you must end all activity on your side such as any kind of judgments. 'You', with all types of different activities subtle or obvious, are the sound in the mind which blocks silence coming into being; and when 'you' come to an end in any direction then silence is.

Letter#43
May 06, 2013

"We think we are going to the future and this is the illusion. In reality, the future is coming to us. And, to live in the "now", this illusion must end. From the day we were born, we have always been here in the "now" without any such movement to the future."

Time
What is time? There is obviously the physical chronological time which is the physical movement in the universe. The movement from here to there, or from LA to New York. Such very movement itself is the physical time. Such physical time has a physical direction such as, from west to east, right to left, south to north or clockwise...etc. Such time is real because the movement in the universe is real, thus there is not much to question about this kind of physical time. It is there, just as the universe is there.

And, there is another kind of time which is very subtle. It is neither a physical movement nor it has a physical direction like the above described physical time. It is a movement in the psyche, and this movement has a direction as **from the past into the future**. What is this movement? This is another kind of time movement we perceive, and let's call it the **psychological time**. We perceive a time passing, and that is why we sometimes say time passes so quickly. We perceive this passing of time like a river with a direction of from the past into the future. Is our perception of a psychological time which is independent from the physical time a reality or an illusion? Or, there is only the physical movement in the universe, and that naturally creates the movement of physical time, and there is no psychological time as a movement from the past into the future at all. This is an important question to inquire into, because we live by such feeling of a time movement from the past into the future. We perceive life like we are in a boat which is in a movement to the future, therefore future becomes very important for us, but if such movement is a total illusion, and if we discover that then we will be left only with the "now" without a past and future. This will mean a totally different kind of perception of life. It will be a new life all together, because we will see that the boat we are in which is called "now" is always in the now without a movement into the future, but with a totally different movement into the now from moment to moment . Then, with such perception, our lives will take place only in the now.

To find the truth of this matter, we have to investigate deeper into the nature of psychological time. What is this time which we sense as a movement from the past to the future? Can it be the accumulation or the growing of the self or the ego? The self at year 1,3,10,20,25, 25.2,25.3...etc. This is a movement from age zero which is birth to the time of death. Accumulation of memory in one's mind as experiences build up the self. So, there is the physical movement of the universe, and there is a "self" in human mind which perceives and translates this movement into another kind of movement from the past into the future. So, the universe has its movement with a physical direction like west to east, and this very physical movement makes the **self** feel like it is moving into the future getting closer and closer to its death.

As time is a movement, we have to go into the question of movement. What is movement? Movement implies change of location. On the physical plane, it is going from coordinate X in universe to coordinate Y. And, on the so called psychological plane, it is going from yesterday to tomorrow or next week since movement must have a direction which means it is west to east, right to left or clockwise etc. on the physical plane; and from the past into the future in the so called psychological plane. The physical movement to cover

the distance between LA and NY is real. Let's say it is 4,000Km.
There must be a physical movement to cover this distance, and your
body actually moves from one point of coordinate which is LA to
another which is NY. But, is the movement in the psychological
plane in this same journey from LA to NY as real as the physical
movement? Let's say the journey is around 4 hours, and you left LA
at 5pm and arrived NY at 9pm. We sense a time moving like a river
from 5pm to 9pm, don't we? Is this perception real? Or, there is no
such time movement from 5pm to 9pm, but the very physical
movement itself covers the distance from 5pm to 9tm rather than a
time movement from the past to the future covering it. In another
words, there was no movement into the future in this journey, but
only a physical movement with a physical direction always in the
now. Let's look at it closer to make it a bit more clear. There seems
to be two independent movements in this journey. One is, I moved
from LA to NY on the physical dimension; and the other is, I also
moved from 5pm to 9pm on the so called time dimension. The
physical movement from LA to NY is real, but in reality, there is no
time travel as from 5pm to 9pm. The very physical movement
naturally creates and covers the distance between 5pm to 9pm. It is
like a natural byproduct rather than an independent reality as we
falsely think. All the journey took place in the now. There was only
the physical movement taking place in this journey, and that very
physical movement was the physical time which was moving from
5pm to 9pm with a physical direction of clockwise or from west to
east as the plane moves. There was no time movement with a
direction from the past into the future, but the mind thinks there is,
and that is the illusion. The only time movement in this journey was
the physical time with a physical direction. The other time which we
think there is with a direction from the past into future exists only in
the human mind. It does not exist in objective reality. There is the
memory of me in LA, and the memory of the 4 hour flight which is
the past, and now I am in NY; and I look at that past, and I create
the illusion of 'me' moving in time from the past to the future. This
perception is unreal. The very physical movement is naturally
bringing the future into the now, and not the now is in a movement
towards a future. When I walk from the living room to the kitchen, I
do not walk towards future, but my very physical movement from the
living room to the kitchen is naturally creating a future to be pulled

into the now. But, **the now** was always the now without any movement to the future. So there is 'the now' only as a dimension, not as a part of a time river which flows from the past to the future. Objects physically move in this dimension of 'now', and this very movement brings the future into the 'now' rather than the now moving into the future as we falsely perceive.

Basically, we sense two different but simultaneous time movements attached to the same physical movement of a physical object in the physical plane. Let's take a 5 minute movement of a truck for instance. Think of this movement as the only movement in the universe for a second, meaning the universe has begun and ended within this 5 minutes only in which the truck moved in empty space. And, let's say there is a human brain observing this movement. There is the actual movement of the truck on the physical plane which is from east to west. This very movement of that truck itself, or the very truck itself can be considered as the same movement of the minute hand of a clock of an infinite size; which means the movement of that truck is exactly the same movement of the clock which is physical movement only. The only difference is one moves in a flat plane of east to west, and the other in a clockwise round plane, but they are exactly the same thing at the infinity level where the flat movement is no different from the clockwise. They are both physical movements and nothing else; whereas our minds have attached an illusory movement to the clock on the wall which has a flow from the past into the future, but this flow is not attached to the movement of that truck. In another words, when we look at the truck moving, the first thing we feel is not a movement into the future but the truck moving to the west; whereas that sense of a time flow into the future is the first thing we feel when we look at the clock on the wall. This subtle attachment which is attributed to the clock as a movement from the past into the future is the very illusion which is at the origin of all human conflict. That clock absolutely has no difference from the truck in terms of movement. They are both physical movements only. So, let's get back to the 5 minute observation of the movement of the truck again. In reality, the truck moves in the timeless eternal moment of the 'now' with no time river from the past into the future involved; but when this movement is observed by a human brain then it is recorded as memory in the brain cells. What happens in this recording process? The observer in the brain feels like it is moving into the future when the truck begins its movement to the west. It is an illusion caused by relativity similar like the one when you feel like you are moving in traffic jam, when in fact, you are not but the car next to you is. The observer records the movement from the beginning, and it looks back and remembers the beginning through memory, and it feels like it is moving to an end; whereas this movement in the psyche which we named as the psychological time is unreal. It does not exist in reality. The only real movement in this 5 minute scene is the movement of the truck which is the physical time, and the very movement of the recording process in the brain becomes the false perception of a time flow into the future. Then, the question which naturally arises is; 'Can the mind observe the outer physical world without the observer interfering with the observation'? Can there be memory recording, which is necessary to function, without a center as the 'I' being formed? The observer of the brain is the movement of psychological time itself, and the ending of the observer is the ending of time of this illusory kind. Then, the mind frees itself from the river of time to experience life with a timeless quality from moment to moment, and not as a **continuous** movement flowing from the past into the future. Then, each moment is met anew with eyes freed from the past, and this means seeing one's wife or husband or the marvelous view of the sea there always like the first time like one has never seen before. Then, life itself becomes an astonishingly interesting journey because such way of rejuvenation by each moment reveals the secret of life in a mysterious way which can not be described by words. And, this is the only way of opening the door to that which is timeless and beyond the **continuity** of time.

Let's analyze this travel from LA to NY more deeply. This is a physical movement with a physical direction which is from the west to the east. A physical object moves from one point in universe to another. The direction of the movement is from the west to east. There is a physical distance to be covered in this movement, and it is measured based on the velocity of the object by a measurement device called the chronological watch which is the physical time. All this is real. Now, there is also another kind of movement in the mind of the person who takes this journey. 'I' took the flight in LA, 'I' had certain experiences in the 4 hour flight, and 'I' am now in New York. 'I' was 4 hours ago, 'I' am now, and 'I' will be; past moving into the future. So, the 'I' moved from the past to the future in this 4 hour journey through the accumulating process of the memory gathered in these four hours. This movement, which the 'I' thinks it is in, has no physical direction like from east to west, but it has a direction of **from the past into the future**. Is this movement as real as the physical movement of the body moving from LA to NY; from west to east? There is the physical chronological clock which moved, shifted or covered a distance of 4 hours in this journey, and this movement is real with a clock moving in a physical clockwise direction. The 4 hours is the physical distance travelled from west to east. And, in this same journey, there is also a psychological clock which moved, shifted or covered another kind of 4 hours. This 4 hours is on the psychological plane. It is 4 hours added to the self or ego scale by the memory recording process of the experiences of this flight as; 'I' was 4 hours ago, and 'I' am now. It is basically a distance of 4 hours as a recorded personal experience which can exist only in the memory cells. The direction of the movement of this psychological clock is from the past into the future. The very movement of this clock is the very movement of **the self, the observer or the ego**. This clock is the **self**. With each ticking minute of the physical clock, the psychological clock moves as well, adding 1 more minute as a static dead distance of memory record as **the self**. This very psychological adding or accumulation is the movement of the psychological clock as the 'the me'. Now, the question is, is this psychological clock real like the physical clock, or is it a total illusion, a wrong perception of the mind? If it is an illusion, and if this illusion is perceived, then what takes place? Then, psychological clock stops all together. And, this frees the mind from time of this kind; therefore the mind perceives the timeless present, and lives only in the present. It is not then a choice for the mind to live in the present; there is absolutely no effort wasted with the techniques of living in the present either, but the very insight which stops the psychological time opens the door naturally to life in the present moment only. Then, there is only the physical time moving clockwise without any psychological one moving from the past into the future. Then there is only one plane to live, and that is the physical life. The plane of psychological life comes to an end. Then, the mind perceives the boat we are in as the 'present' which is not a part of a time movement as the past, present and the future; but only **the present**. The boat which is called 'now', and which we think is carrying us in the river of time into the future stops all of a sudden with this insight. And, what we are left with then is only the 'now', and since we perceived we are not moving into a future, future loses all its effect, pressure and importance in our lives. What becomes important and the only thing is the present then. If we think we are moving to somewhere, then that somewhere which we think we are moving towards becomes naturally very important, but if we discover that in reality we are not moving towards anywhere, but always here, then naturally that 'here and now' becomes all important. After such insight, a future destination disappears leaving us only with the now. Then, naturally the very journey itself in the now becomes all important, and not the destination. Then, the now is perceived as a timeless dimension rather than a part of time as the past, present and future. Present then is not the final point arrived in the river of time coming from the past moving into the future, but it becomes a dimension which contains all past and future, all beginning and end. The river of time disappears or dissolves into the timelessness of the present.

So, this psychological time can exist only in human mind which has a recorded memory as the past, and a self or an observer which looks at this past, and from that past projects a future into which it is moving. Without the self, or the observer where is such time movement? Let's say before human beings came to this earth, was there time as a movement from the past to the future? Or, was there only the physical movement of things in the present moment? Think of a tree long before human beings came to this earth. The tree comes into being, it grows and it withers away after some time. This might take, let's say 100 years. But, without an observer which records the life time of this tree, where is time as a movement from the past to the future? The tree lives in the present moment. This living takes 100 years. Time as a static measurable distance like 100 years is real, but is there a time movement which is independent from the physical movement to cover this 100 years distance, or the physical movement itself creates and covers this distance naturally? So, without any recorded memory of the life of this ancient tree, thus without an observer, there is no time as a movement into the future from a past; but there is only living of the tree in the present moment, and this very living which is the physical movement is the only reality which is physical time, and there is no such thing as a psychological time.

There is only the physical, chronological time which is the physical movement itself, and since physical movement is relative, time is relative. There is no absolute time independent from the physical movement in the universe. Time is relative based on the physical movement of the universe. If all the physical movement in the universe is frozen for a moment, then all sense of time comes to an end. This includes the illusory psychological time in human mind as well because the self which is thought is also of the material brain in its physical movement. If there were an absolute sense of time, then it would go on independent of the frozen physical movement of the universe.

If human mind with its observer at its center is removed from life, then what remains as reality is the universe in its physical movement, and this reality knows no past and future. Universe knows only the "now". Time as a movement from the past to the future is an illusionary invention or wrong perception of the human mind, and because of such wrong perception past and future becomes extraordinarily important; whereas the only reality in the universe is the present. The reality is not a scale of the past, present and the future, because then the present becomes an unimportant part of the river of time. The reality is; 'there is only the present which is totally free from the past and the future'. This very moment will not be a dead memory of the past two minutes later, because that would imply this moment is the continuity of the past; and this is the illusion. This moment is eternally alive totally free from both the past and the future.

We think we are going to the future and this is the illusion. In reality, the future is coming to us. And, to live in the "now", this illusion must end. From the day we were born, we have always been here in the "now" without any such movement to the future."

Practical suggestions on time and living in the present moment:

-Be aware that in the journey of life you feel like you are on a boat which is carrying you on the river of time from the past into the future. Question whether such perception is a real one or an illusion all together.

- There is the present moment as the dimension of all existence in the universe. This present moment is non-movement in terms of time flowing from the past into the future. So, why do we sense such a time movement then? It is because the brain is recording the physical movement in the world that takes place in the present moment, and that very recording itself is the illusion of time we sense which seems to be this flow because the brain perceives this movement to be a continuous one rather than a totally new birth of each moment. There is the 'recorded' as the past, and the 'will be recorded' as the future and the very recording process becomes the machinery of time movement. But, such recording takes place only in the brain as the observer; therefore such time can exist as an illusion only in that brain, not in the reality of the universe. And, for the brain to perceive the timeless movement of the present, it must be freed from this area of time all together. The recording is about the recording of the story of the 'me, self or ego' with its past and future, and the very ending of the ego is the ending of that time process as a movement from the past into the future. Only then, the mind can enter into the dimension of the present moment totally. Memory recording will continue because we couldn't function otherwise, but then there will be recording just like a camera which records without forming a center as the 'I'.

Letter#44
July 18, 2013

"Isn't the moment of the touch of true happiness supreme form of spirituality? Which ritual, religion, method, savior...etc can offer such highest form of spiritual feeling of the moment of joy touching one's soul at great depths of one's being and dispelling all darkness by the light of that touch?"

The moment of true happiness is the moment of true spirituality

What is the relationship of spirituality and happiness? Can one be spiritual without happiness, or can one be happy without spirituality? What does it mean to be spiritual, and what does it mean to be truly happy?

Spirituality implies something beyond the material things of the world. Being able to find nothing in the material world which gave them a true sense of fulfillment in life, human beings began seeking something beyond the material, and this is where things began to get complicated because what is beyond the material is unknown for the one who stands on the shores of the known material world. So, how is one to bridge the known to the unknown? Humanity has invented many spiritual practices, methods, religions, saviors etc. in order to make this bridge to reach the shores of the unknown, but seeing humanity in its current miserable state, one can conclude that apparently none of these have worked properly. Can the known be bridged to the unknown? Or, any attempt to bridge the two is simply an impossibility, because they are two different worlds or dimensions? In order to bridge two things, they must somehow be of the same material existing in the same dimension; whereas the spiritual is beyond the material world, and only with the total ending of the material things of the world the other may begin. So these two can not be bridged, but the very ending of the one may become the beginning of the other.

Is happiness to be reached at the end? Can one reach happiness by practicing certain spiritual methods, beliefs..etc for some time, and then reach happiness? This implies spirituality and happiness are two different things; spirituality being the means to happiness. Or, happiness is discovered only by walking through the tunnel of unhappiness which is the actuality of what one is. The very walking through that tunnel is understanding oneself through self observation which is the only true spirituality, and then such spirituality is not a means to some future happiness; but the very first step into this tunnel of understanding oneself becomes also the last step of a joyful discovery. Then, happiness comes unexpectedly in this journey of self knowing, making spirituality and happiness an inseparable whole naturally.

Isn't the moment of the touch of true happiness supreme form of spirituality? Which ritual, religion, method, savior...etc. can offer such highest form of spiritual feeling of the moment of joy touching one's soul at great depths of one's being and dispelling all darkness by the light of that touch?

Practical suggestions on spirituality and happiness:
-Always make sure that happiness sheds light upon your spiritual path rather than any kind of techniques or rituals.
-Always be aware and remember that spirituality and true happiness are an inseparable whole. One can not exist without the other. Know that if your spiritual path is not connecting you to the source of all joy, then you are on the wrong path.

Letter#45
October 15, 2013

"We enjoy something, and in that moment we forget all our problems by losing ourselves in the beauty of the thing we enjoy. Then, the mind begins seeking that enjoyment we have had in which there was total self forgetfulness, and this is where the problem begins. Can we simply just enjoy the things of life without being attached like we are a short term guest in this world?"

Enjoyment without being attached
What is enjoyment? It's dictionary meaning is 'the state of taking pleasure in something'; the enjoyment of a nice walk in nature, watching a beautiful sunset or the splendid stars of a quiet evening, or being with the loved ones etc. Is there anything wrong in such enjoyment? Obviously not, because without such enjoyment of life we would be dead livings.

There is also attachment involved in enjoyment. We enjoy something, and in that moment we forget all our problems by losing ourselves in the beauty of the thing we enjoy. Then, the mind begins seeking that enjoyment we have had in which there was total self forgetfulness, and this is where the problem begins. As long as there is enjoyment of something without making it into an escape from our problems, there is no problem at all. On the contrary, it is very healthy to enjoy things of life as we are living things. So, the problem begins the moment the mind makes that thing we enjoy into an attachment. This means it is not pure enjoyment anymore, but an escape of the mind from its turmoil and misery.

What is wrong then with being attached to the thing we have had enjoyed? Attachment is a process of formation of a bond which has its roots in the past memories of the things we have enjoyed. So firstly, attachment bond is rooted in the past, therefore it denies true enjoyment which can take place only in the present moment. The very first enjoyment of a thing is free from the past, and it is totally rooted in the present only; but the moment attachment bond is formed and the mind begins to seek this enjoyment of the very first time through this bond, then we can never have that original feeling of enjoyment we have had in the first time. It is simply because now the past memories will be meeting that present scene of enjoyment, and the past meeting the present will deny living totally in the present moment, thus that original quality of enjoyment will never be there as long as the past memories of the attachment bond seek that quality. So, the formation of the attachment bond for something we truly enjoyed will prevent us having that original quality of enjoyment next time we are in the same scenery. This is one reason why attachment is dangerous and destructive to enjoyment.

Another reason why attachment will be harmful to the original quality of enjoyment is the very motive of being attached which implies seeking pleasure. We get attached to things because we get pleasure of some kind, or a feeling of security, or a sense of self forgetfulness, but then that thing becomes an escape for us from our misery, rather than being a thing of true enjoyment. When we are attached to something which offers us such an escape from ourselves, then pain becomes inevitable because there is always the risk of losing that thing we are attached to since nothing is permanent; and this causes fear. So, fear of losing together with the actuality of losing the thing we are attached to is the beginning of suffering. This means pain and pleasure are inseparable within the attachment bond. There is no such a thing as an attachment bond which contains only pleasure within itself without pain. Attachment bond will absolutely contain both pleasure and pain like the two inseparable sides of one coin.

So, what is one to do then? What would be the wise way of enjoying life without any suffering involved? It seems, one must live and enjoy things of life without being attached. This demands extraordinary quality of awareness to the activities of the mind which has such great tendency to get attached. One must be very watchful of the mind in its operations of forming the attachment bond. One must go deeper to understand the ways of the mind while operating in the formation of such bond. Only in such deep understanding freedom from attachment can come, and this is true meditation.

How can one be attached to the things of the past memories of pleasure and live totally in the present moment? It is an impossibility. To be able to totally live in the present, one must be free from all attachment with its past memories. Only in such total freedom from all attachment, the mind can truly be in touch with the present. Otherwise, one will be living in the river of time all one's life while one is talking about living in the present all the time. The very movement of attachment itself in the psyche is the movement of time.

The question then becomes, "Can one enjoy the things of life in the present moment, and die to it once it is over without making an image in the mind of the original quality of that enjoyment, and then seeking that image to have it again"? If the mind can die this way without making an image of memory which then forms the attachment bond, then each time one meets that enjoyment scene, that meeting will have the fresh quality of the original enjoyment just like the very first time without any residues of the past which distort the direct perception of beauty in the present moment. So, enjoyment can take place only in the present moment without any interference of the past memories which build the attachment bond.

Practical suggestions on enjoyment without being attached:
-Enjoy things of life like without being attached like you are a short term guest in this world.

-Do not depend your happiness on the things you enjoy. Enjoy the thing, and die to it once it is over.

-Be aware of your mind's attempt to make the thing of enjoyment into an attachment which is built up by the past memories of the actual moment of enjoyment.

- Every time you are about to do the thing you are most attached to like logging onto your facebook account, watching a movie, eating your favorite food etc. stop for 10 full seconds, and just simply watch your desire in this time gap by closely being aware of it in silence. Don't control, suppress or judge your desire; but just simply look at it and see it clearly. That's it. If you can do this, then you will see that 10 seconds of time gap will be the ground where silent intelligence will start flowering, and the beginning of that flowering will be the beginning of the ending of that attachment. Then, you can be engaged with the same activity if necessary with a free mind, rather than one which is enslaved by that attachment. Start it now, because most probably you are going to do something you are attached to soon after reading this.

-Ask yourself this question to meditate upon; "Can I easily take a holiday for a week in a place where internet and mobile phones are not allowed"?

Letter#46
November 6, 2013

"So, self knowledge is the process of inward purification. And, to know yourself, you just need to look at yourself in the mirror of relationship, and see yourself as you actually are without any judgments or condemnations."

Inward purification

Can there be a spiritual life without a process of inward purification? And, what does it mean to purify oneself inwardly? Is there anything pure within oneself spiritually? Does love have a pure quality, or is it mixed with other things like jealousy, ambition, sorrow, loneliness etc? Are we pure as we are now?

First, let's see whether we are pure as we are now or not. One of the dictionary meanings of the word 'pure' is 'clean and free from harmful substances'. Are we inwardly totally clean and free from harmful substances? What are harmful substances inwardly? Can anger, fear, hatred, jealousy, envy, comparison, ambition, suffering, loneliness be some of those harmful substances inwardly? If they are, and if they are in us, then we are not pure inwardly. Can love exist in impurity, or love can flourish only in pure soil? If such purity is necessary for a truly spiritual life, then how can we cleanse ourselves from such qualities which cause the impurity?

Let's for instance take one quality which blurs the pure waters, and that is hatred. How can there be a process of inward purification or inward cleansing from hatred? Can any method, technique, ritual, belief, so called sacred book, religion cleanse our hearts from this quality, or we simply have to do our own job without depending on anything outside, but our own light of understanding and observation only? Surely, there is only one way, and that is being a light unto ourselves. We prefer to be very lazy when it comes to inward matters, and we generally choose the easy way like believing in a religion, or applying some certain quick spiritual methods invented by the latest guru; but the absolute fact is we must do the cleaning job of our house by ourselves, and there are no short cuts to it. If we wait for an outside agency to do it for us, then we will have to wait forever. No book, no savior, no religion, no ritual, no spiritual technique can start this purification process. One can do this purification only by watching, questioning, observing and understanding oneself. So, self knowledge is the process of inward purification; and to know yourself, you just need to look at yourself in the mirror of relationship and see yourself as you actually are without any judgments or condemnations. How can a technique, ritual, belief, savior, or a so called sacred book cleanse the hatred in your heart? Only awareness, watchfulness and the understanding the roots of such hatred at great depths will wipe out all hatred at once. This is the only way for inward spiritual purification, and without such purification process of the heart, all so called spirituality will have little meaning other than mere entertainment.

Practical suggestions on inward purification:

-Just simply be aware of the impurity within you without any effort to be pure.

Letter#47
February 6, 2014

"The eagle in its free flight is not concerned about death or security. The eagle is concerned only about the beauty of the free flight in the present moment, and there is no death or insecurity for the eagle in its flight in the present moment. That free flight in the present which knows no death or insecurity is the gateway opening to immortality."

The fact of Impermanence and Insecurity

There is neither security in life, nor permanence. An earthquake or another catastrophic event can come and wipe away everything. This is an absolute fact. After all, there is death at the end waiting for us all as the final and absolute wiping away of all that we have gathered in this world. This very fact of impermanence caused by death is the ultimate feeling of insecurity for us. So, insecurity and impermanence are the absolute facts of life. The root of human suffering and unhappiness is the conflict that arises from human non-acceptance of these absolute facts; thus the battle that goes on all the time between the fact of what is, and what we desire it to be. It is like not accepting the fact of sun rising from the east, and seeking ways to make it rise from the west. This non-acceptance of an unchangeable fact is the cause of conflict; therefore unhappiness. In the same way, the very seeking of psychological security is an illusion exactly same like seeking ways to make the sun rise from the west. Wouldn't one's life be wasted in perpetual conflict if one could not accept the fact of sun rising from the east? In the same way, unless we fully accept the fact of insecurity in life, and stop seeking psychological security through gathering things of the world, then our lives will be wasted in perpetual conflict. We might get a certain sense of relative psychological security through owning a big house, a good bank account or a husband, but the ultimate fact is all those things are impermanent; therefore there is no real feeling of absolute security to be reached by seeking it through the transient things of the material world. Our futile efforts of gathering material wealth in order to find such security creates nothing but a sense of further emptiness of insecurity that needs to be filled with more material things of the world which then becomes a desperate vicious circle with no way out. The more one gathers, the more one is filled with the fear of losing all those that are gathered; which means, the more one gathers, the more one is pulled towards inner darkness. The very motive to gather more is in fact the very futile attempt to escape from the fact of insecurity of life into an illusory feeling of security. And, this attempt in itself is no different from the attempt of trying to make the sun rise from the west. It is simply impossible, illusory and the very root of perpetual conflict. The only rational and sane security that should be sought is the physical security needed for the survival of the physical body, and this must be provided; but apart from that, any other seeking of security in the psychological realm of the 'I', or the 'ego' is a total illusion which is indeed at the very root of all human conflict.

There is one true unshakable feeling of inner security though, and that can only come through the intelligent understanding and acceptance of such fact of insecurity and impermanence as qualities inherently embedded in life. When one simply, peacefully and truly accepts these facts of life, then conflict ends; hence there comes a burst of inward energy. Then, one does not get attached to things, but rather simply enjoys the things in life with the wisdom of a temporary guest who is taking a journey to this beautiful world. Then, naturally there is a sense of thrill, danger and adventure in one's life simply because one lives totally with the fact of insecurity and impermanence. This very sense of dangerous living with no seeking of any psychological security makes one feel fully alive in each and every single cell. That is why, generally at times of youth, when one lives adventurously one feels free, fresh, happy and alive; and the moment one begins to seek psychological security at later ages, one is being buried while alive. The very seeking of psychological security is also the absolute denial of living in the present, because how can one be concerned about psychological security in the future while one totally lives in the present.

The majestic river of life is like the wildest horse which can never be tamed, and you can only enjoy the ride when you accept fully the fact of dangerously adventurous spirit of life which gives a unique beauty to the experience of living. There is no other way, but intelligent acceptance of the fact of danger element in life which means accepting the fact that nothing is really under our control. The real and full acceptance of this fact deep down within ourselves is the beginning of true peace and wisdom.

The eagle in its free flight is not concerned about death or security. The eagle is concerned only about the beauty of the free flight in the present moment, and there is no death or insecurity for the eagle in its flight in the present moment. That free flight in the present which knows no death or insecurity is the gateway opening to immortality.

Practical suggestions on the fact of Impermanence and Insecurity:

-Live your life with a spirit of danger and adventure without seeking any sense of psychological security like you are falling down a cliff. Do not seek anything to hold on to in this free fall because you will get terribly hurt if you attempt to get attached at high speed of such falling. Just enjoy the beautiful scenery each and every moment of this journey of free fall until you hit the ground. Life is all about fully enjoying this free fall until the very last second of hitting the ground. You will miss the whole point of living if you are concerned about the moment of hitting the ground or what happens afterwards. Just enjoy the fall at the exact altitude you are without thinking about the lower or higher altitudes.

FIND YOUR SECRET KEY

DICTIONARY
by Memo Ozdogan

www.facebook.com/FindYourSecretKey

Wisdom: Light of joy combined with the intelligence of love and inward simplicity. Laughter from the heart.
Synonym: Joy, love, simplicity

Spiritual: The one who lives with the light of love and compassion of the heart. The one who is falling in love with life itself; rather than with the things of life. The one who seeks the truth of life through free questioning rather than through certain rituals or methods.
Synonym: Free, joyful, wise, lover

Love: The unknown which no words can describe. That which is beyond all measurement, and without a beginning and an end. The timeless ecstasy of the present moment. The original source of unlimited life energy. The heart of true spirituality. The eternal flame that sheds light upon darkness.
Synonym: Light, joy, beauty, compassion, eternal, freedom

Philosopher: Philosophia means 'Love of Sophia'; which means 'Love of Wisdom' in Greek as 'Sophia' means 'Wisdom' in Greek. And, philosopher means the one who himself has fallen in love with Sophia by igniting an eternal fire of love in his heart for Sophia rather than merely repeating others' love stories of Sophia. Such love of Sophia is the very meaning of life, and such lover is the flower. Each human being must be, and can be such a lover of Sophia and flower in the only true meaning of life. The deepest secrets of creation are to be found in that love.
Synonym: Lover of wisdom

Angel: A human being who is totally free from the ego; therefore capable of loving unconditionally.
Synonym: Enlightened, lover

God: An illusionary idea of 'a creator separate from the created' which humans of the planet earth believed in because of their fear of life and of death at the era of ignorance. The false denial of the oneness in life through the division of the creator and the created. Beyond the illusion of this idea may lie something truly sacred.
Synonym: Life, love

Loser: A person who worships only the material things of the world like money and power; therefore who inevitably misses the whole point of the journey of life which is the light of joyful living and love. Synonym: Blind

FIND YOUR SECRET KEY

PRACTICAL TIPS FOR LIVING
by Memo Ozdogan

www.facebook.com/FindYourSecretKey

EAT WHEN YOU ARE HUNGRY

Eat whenever you feel hungry just as much to feed your hunger, but make sure with a few minutes of silent observation that the hunger signals are coming from your stomach rather than your mind. There is nothing wrong to eat when the biological body wants it, but if you listen very carefully to the voice of the body you will see that the biological body needs little food whereas the mind needs much more. So, there is no need to control our eating with special diets. Such controlling will only further the conflict of eating, but just become aware whether it is the body or the mind which is eating, and such awareness will make the best diet for us naturally and easily.

FREEDOM FROM THE TIME EFFECT

As long as time has its effect on you, you cannot live fully in the present moment. Be aware of your changing moods on certain labeled days of the week such as Friday, Saturday or Monday...etc. In reality, there is no such labeling of any given day. Each day is simply a day. We need these labels in order to make plan and function, but see how our mood depends so much on these labels of days, and free yourself from them. As long as our mood is affected by such labeling, we will inevitably be enslaved by time, and therefore we will not be able to enter into the stillness of the present moment with its peace and joy. Just simply be aware of this kind of time effect on your mind, and this awareness will begin to free your mind from such time effect.

EACH LIMITED EDITION DAY IS UNIQUIE

Take each day of your life as a uniquely limited edition piece, and shape each one of your days like a skilled jeweler handcrafting a masterpiece with great love and attention, as each day will be the brick with which you will be building your eternal house. The beauty of your eternal house depends on the beauty of the pieces that make it.

PLAYING WITH THE EGO

Play games with your ego by inviting certain situations in which the ego will feel ashamed, desiring, angry, fearful, lustful, humiliated, etc. Basically, invite all the emotions and feelings, and watch the ego from all these different angles. For instance, if you have a friend who looks down on you, try spending some time with that person as a spiritual exercise, and watch the ego in its reactions. Since you have deliberately invited such an occasion awareness will be growing on the background; therefore you won't get harmed. Try pushing it more to the limits each time with greater awareness, and you will see this will help you to grow so much inwardly. After some time, the ego will begin liking this spiritual exercise, because it will soon realize it gets great strength by going beyond itself to the higher levels of knowledge through such exercise. Be aware of this too. Then, the ego will say, "Who is being aware? It is also me". Be aware of this as well. Just watch, and you will find yourself in laughter sometimes in this fun game with the ego, and that laughter will be signs of joyful wisdom coming into existence unexpectedly and unknowingly at the moments of watchfulness without a watcher anymore as the ego.

ENERGY REFLECTION

If you feel your energy is being sucked by someone with bad intentions in a business meeting or elsewhere, just simply stay silent for a few seconds by focusing on a point in the room until you feel such sucking stops. This non-action of focusing on a single point quietly will act as a mirror which will reflect the vampire like energy waves coming from that person back to him or her. This way, you will preserve your energy and the other person will begin sucking his or her own energy instead of yours.

EASY TIPS TO PREVENT CANCER

-Walk regularly, and live close to nature if possible.
-Try to stay away from stress at all costs.
-Do not keep things inside you, but rather express them openly. Never keep hatred in your heart. Jesus wisely said, "If you bring forth what is within you, what you bring forth will save you. If you do not bring forth what is within you, what you do not bring forth will destroy you."
-Avoid eating non-organic and genetically modified foods. Try to have a vegetarian diet as much as possible. If you have to eat meat, reduce the red meat amount to the very minimum, and occasionally ask yourself why you eat meat. Do not be overweight.
-Do not consume excessive amounts of alcohol. Prefer red wine if you drink.

-Do not smoke. Smoke less and very light if you have to. If you do, you must heal the body from the effects with an exercise in nature therapy.

-Do not forget that the best antidote for cancer virus is joy of love in your heart.

THE FREE FALL

Live your life with a spirit of danger and adventure without seeking any sense of psychological security like you are falling down a cliff. Do not seek anything to hold on to in this free fall because you will get terribly hurt if you attempt to get attached at high speed of such falling. Just enjoy the beautiful scenery each and every moment of this journey of free fall until you hit the ground. Life is all about fully enjoying this free fall until the very last second of hitting the ground. You will miss the whole point of living if you are concerned about the moment of hitting the ground or what happens afterwards. Just enjoy the fall at the exact altitude you are without thinking about the lower or higher altitudes which means living in the present.

MIRROR MEDITATION AND AURA PERCEPTION

Spend some time looking at the mirror sometimes when you are not in rush. Just look at the mirror, and see your physical body. Then, look at your eyes in the mirror very attentively, and try to see the 'you, yourself, or ego" through your eyes in the mirror. Be aware that both your physical body and your ego are reflected on the mirror. To see your ego on the mirror demands a silent and deep looking like that of a baby's. Just look in deep silence and you will begin to see this living 'you' on the mirror just like you see your physical body. If you do this mirror meditation sometimes, you will realize that after a period of time self awareness will be sharpened. This very ability to see your persona or self on the mirror is the ability to see the Aura. The more this ability is sharpened through such self awareness, the more clearly the auras are perceived. When once this ability begins growing within you, then you will naturally get more and more acutely sensitive to perceive people's auras instantly. This means you will see their true self behind the masks immediately without taking time which will naturally prevent you wasting your time with some people who have extremely subtle masks.

I EAT TOO MUCH

Unless your weight is too low or you are suffering from certain specific problems of gaining weight, then make a mantra to yourself by saying **"I eat too much"** after each meal you have; it does not matter how much you eat. Very often there is a truth to this both because we generally eat more than the body needs as human body is originally designed to survive with very little but right food, and also because we are aging by each passing day; therefore we must eat less and less. If you repeat this mantra of **"I eat too much"** after each meal by seeing the truth of it, then an awareness will grow, and you will see by time you will begin eating less and less naturally without making any effort or conflict of diets . You must see the truth of it though for this to work as otherwise you will deceive yourself. Looking at and being aware of even a tiny little bit of fat particles in any part of your body will help you to see the truth of eating too much because our bodies must have zero amount of **excess** fat below the skin. Such excess implies the subtle existence of the ego in action.

1 MINUTE OF PRESENCE

Right now, after reading this, can you come into the presence of this moment for about 1 minute? Just simply get out of any rush you are in and relax; then stop all inward activity which is thinking as well as any outward activity you might be engaged in, and be silently aware of the physical space you are in. Just look quietly around, and be aware of the objects that fill the space. See their shapes, colors etc. Look attentively at any little detail which you never looked at before carefully. Be present and aware like this one minute is the only time period of the life you are having. This means no past and no future. You will also feel a sense of time slowing down in this 1 minute period. Presence in the now slows down the river of time, and through the door of such slowing down of time, peace begins to come in. Do this sometimes to open the door more and more.

ATTACHMENT AWARENESS

Every time you are about to do the thing you are most attached to like logging onto your facebook account, watching a movie, eating your favorite food etc. stop for 10 full seconds, and just simply watch your desire in this time gap by closely being aware of it in silence.

Don't control, suppress or judge your desire; but just simply look at it and see it clearly. That's it. If you can do this, then you will see that 10 seconds of time gap will be the ground where silent intelligence will start flowering, and the beginning of that flowering will be the beginning of the ending of that attachment. Then, you can be engaged with the same activity if necessary with a free mind, rather than one which is enslaved by that attachment. Start it now, because most probably you are going to do something you are attached to soon after reading this.

WATCH THE GREEN
Spending time in nature has a great healing effect both physically and psychologically as well. It is good to go for a hike in nature as much as possible for instance. One must also be alone sometimes in nature for better communication with nature and for better healing effects. You will hear the joyful singing of mother nature better when you spend some time alone in her compassionate hands. If somehow one does not have much time, or one feels lazy for a hike, then even watching the green of nature has healing and silencing effect on the mind. Watch that green silently as much as possible. Even 10 minutes each day if possible will make a lot of difference for the mind to become silent and peaceful. Just watch quietly.

WATCH THE THINKER
Watch the thinker in your mind closely, and you will realize at that moment a higher level of consciousness will be activated. When there is such watchfulness of the thinker thought will slow down, and this very watching of the thinker will be the entrance door to the dimension of meditation. Then, you will begin to go into the deeper states of meditation when you begin also to watch the watcher. In this journey towards your inner depths with such flowering of meditation, there comes a moment when the division between the thinker or the watcher and the watched disappears; leaving the mind in an awakened state of bliss without a center, and therefore without a periphery. And, this state is the universal unity or the ultimate truth with its unshakable peace and joy.

VITAMIN PILLS
Do not take vitamin pills unless there is an absolute medical

necessity. It is most likely that the lack of physical energy you feel is caused by the psyche. If there is not enough peace in the mind with its vital life energy, then the physical body will feel the lack of physical energy. Human body is a very strong ultra-intelligent machine, and if you do not suffer from starvation like those in Africa, then the food you eat will be enough for the body to be strong. Just try eating a variety of different food instead of eating the same thing often. Even those who are poor and who can't have enough variety of food have strong bodies because that is the nature of the body. It can stay strong with little food. In most cases, the lack of physical energy we feel is not because we do not get enough vitamins, but it is because we do not have enough peace and happiness in the mind. Once the mind touches that true peace and happiness, then the body will have explosive physical energy. So, do not harm your livers with such pills. If you feel anything by using such pills, then it is most probably the placebo effect.

FIND YOUR SECRET KEY

PRACTICAL SCHOOL OF SPIRITUALITY
by *Memo Ozdogan*

www.facebook.com/FindYourSecretKey

CLOCK MEDITATION

Take an analog clock or watch, and spare your 5 minutes sometime for clock meditation. Make sure you spare some time when you have no rush for anything. Simply watch the clock in these 5 minutes, and be aware of the time movement silently and passively. What is important is to be deeply aware of the river of time carrying us into the future. Just be aware silently. Be aware of the synchronized movement of the inward clock moving into the future while the outer is moving clockwise. This very silent awareness of the movement of time itself is the awakening of presence in the now. And, you will experience a sense of time slowing down in this silent awareness, and such presence will be the entrance door to a peaceful meditative state of the mind.

THE LOTTERY OF LIFE

There are many in the world who have great difficulty to acquire the basic things of life such as proper food, clothes and shelter, and for them these things are the jackpot. There is also the millionaire whose lottery is perhaps related with being a billionaire. So, this thing of lottery in life is quite a relative thing with a different meaning for each.

One feels though that the real lottery which one won at birth is "life" itself, but very rarely we can see and appreciate this most marvelous lottery we have already won by being born to this world because we are so very lost in the false lotteries which exist within the real eternal one.

WHAT IS AWARENESS?

The sun paints the sky twice a day in brilliant colors, and the moon touches the waters in the deep silence of the night without us noticing such splendid dance of love on earth while we endlessly read books on spiritual awareness and get lost in it. Seeing the beauty is a major part of awareness, but unfortunately we prefer to look for complicated ideas of some strange mystical awareness in many so called spiritual books. To go far in the vast ocean of awareness, one must start with near. How can one possibly voyage into the unfathomable depths of spiritual beauty without first seeing the immense beauty of that sun painting the sky? So, awareness starts with the simple seeing of what is around us outwardly, and then it grows inwardly by seeing what is within us. It is as simple as that though we might desire some strange and complicated ideas of it. Unfortunately, simplicity of living began to look like something stupid in today's world whereas clever complication is seen the right way of living; but in reality, inward simplicity is the truly wise way of living, and complication is the product of a stupified mind lost in excessive thinking.

RECOGNITION OF YOUR EGO

If it were possible to copy and transfer your ego or self into another human body, how easy would it be for you to recognize your ego? Let's say one out of ten artificially made virtual human avatars contains your ego built in his or her brain. How long would it take for you to recognize your ego among them? Could you recognize only by looking and feeling, or would you need to talk a bit to see the character features? An interesting thinking exercise to test how well you know yourself.

TIME

There is the present moment as the dimension of all existence in the universe. This present moment is non-movement in terms of time flowing from the past into the future. So, why do we sense such a time movement then? It is because the brain is recording the physical movement in the world that takes place in the present moment, and that very recording itself is the illusion of time we sense which seems to be this flow because the brain perceives this movement to be a continuous one rather than a totally new birth of each moment. There is the 'recorded' as the past, and the 'will be recorded' as the future and the very recording process becomes the machinery of time movement. But, such recording takes place only in the brain as the observer; therefore such time can exist as an illusion only in that brain, not in the reality of the universe. And, for the brain to perceive the timeless movement of the present, it must be freed from this area of time. The recording is about the recording of the story of the 'me, self or ego' with its past and future, and the very ending of the ego is the ending of that time process as a movement from the past into the future. Only then the mind can enter into the dimension of the present moment totally. Memory recording will continue because we couldn't function otherwise, but then there will be recording just like a camera which records without forming a center as the 'I'.

THE HUMAN TEMPLE

If all those who believe in God would have humans as the object of their worship rather than some images of a dead god, then perhaps the living god could descend upon earth. God in the churches, mosques, temples or so called holy books is dead. Such worship of the dead images of god divides humans, and then they kill one another in the name of such god; never realizing the fact that killing another human being is killing the living god in the name of the dead one. Life that dwells in humanity is the true living temple to be worshipped, and in that temple humanity is one big family with no divisions brought by worshipping of the dead temples. Unless one has a taste of worshipping in this temple by getting lost in the ritual of that mad and true love for another human being, one can never know what truth or true feeling of being spiritual is.

GOING BEYOND THE WORD

Just take a look at these words first,
-God
-Tao
-Divine love
-Universal intelligence
-Buddha consciousness
-Christ
-The Beloved
-Eternal life
-Sacred wisdom
-Nothingness

Those who truly realized something beyond the material realm had to use certain words to communicate that thing beyond. But, all these words are used to point out exactly the same thing which is beyond, and yet our minds have different images associated with all those above words. As long as we have any image of what is beyond through a word we will get stuck in the limitation of that word; whereas truth is beyond the word. Words are needed to communicate, but we must be extremely aware that the word is not the thing it stands for. The word 'door' is not the actuality of the door. Try to wipe away all these above words and the images attached to them from your mind, and just stay with 'no word' that stands for the thing which is beyond the material as that thing beyond must be nameless, formless and beyond all description. But, the moment our minds have a word for that thing, then the mind gets stuck in the word never being able to go beyond.

AMBITION TEST

If you were given the keys to a room which is full of gold, precious diamonds and very high radiation at the same time, would you go in if a minute spent in that room would take away one month from your life? And, if you do how long would you stay in total in that room?

GOODNESS OF LOVE

Can there be spirituality without true natural goodness in one's heart? The attempt to be good because the religions, the gurus or the so called sacred books said so is clearly not the goodness that flowers naturally. It is rather an imposed sense of goodness with very little meaning. Or, can any religious or spiritual ritual open the door to such flowering of love in one's heart? Obviously not; simply because dynamically living quality of love can not be born out of any mechanical repetitive practices. Love must be free from the time bounded cause and effect chain. There are now the new age spiritual movements of many different kinds all around the world where people talk about love endlessly. Goodness can come about only with this flowering of love in the temple of one's heart. When you actually love your friend, your children, animals or the trees; there is neither any cause in that love nor any rituals or the dead words of the so called spiritual books. There simply is causeless love bubbling in your heart. No books including the so called sacred ones, no practices, no beliefs or no words of love can open the door to that mysterious goodness of love.

GET UNDRESSED SPRITUALLY

In the spiritual journey of climbing the mountain of truth, we must leave the entire inward burden behind so that we can feel light inwardly. Just like the simple action of getting undressed in a hot summer day, we should get undressed inwardly with that quality of simplicity without making it into another conflict of the spiritual kind. Attachments are our inward clothes that we hold on to, and the wise and true way of ending attachment with one simple action should be like taking our jacket out in a hot day without any complications involved. Just simply cut it off with one strike without the complications of time being involved. We do not take time and complicate the process of taking out our jacket; we simply take it out. We should also take out our inward jackets just like this with one simple action. If we can not abandon attachments with such simple action, then naturally we will find ourselves in a new conflict of detachment complication in which the mind will get lost again; whereas total freedom of the mind from any sense of conflict is the most essential thing on the path of wisdom. This quality of inward simplicity in action might be the only way to climb the mountain top in our spiritual journey, and when once we are undressed this way inwardly, then the light of the simplicity of inward nakedness will begin radiating.

CRITICAL AWARENESS
When you hear a sincere voice saying, "I do not agree"; listen attentively because that might be truth speaking to you as a signpost showing the right path. Be extremely awake in your desire to listen to sincere critics rather than listening to empty flatteries. While such sincere critics hold the great power to awaken you spiritually, empty flatteries are equally powerful to put you in a deep state of sleep. Critical awareness is the path of spiritual awakening.

THE LAW OF ATTRACTION
The law of attraction is fundamentally about the quality of communication between you and the universe. Just like the radio transmitter, the signals transmitted by you must be strong enough to be clearly received and heard by the universe. The strength and the quality of those signals depend on the quality of your inner psychological energy. If this energy at the source of transmission is strong, then the signals will be clear and strong. The quality of your inner energy depends on your inward clarity. If you eliminated inward conflict of qualities such as jealousy, hatred, fear, feeling of loneliness, attachment, anger etc. then your inner energy becomes

lucid. And, together with right meditation, love with its light of joy begins to radiate at the very origin of your inner energy field. This then, brings about the highest form of energy which will transmit the strongest signals establishing a perfectly flawless connection between you and the universe for the law of attraction to have effect in your life with great precision. It is like getting connected to the central computer of life wirelessly to command certain changes in your life. The better the quality and coherence of the wireless signals sent out, the more the chances that they will be received by the central computer. The key then, is the harmony of love and the light of joy in your inner spiritual life.

WHAT IS ENLIGTHENMENT?
Once a man asked a wise man what enlightenment was? The wise man said, "Imagine you have a stroke now, and you are dead. And, imagine your body came back to life after an hour or so by some miraculous rebirth fully conscious with all the physical senses fully awake, whereas your ego could not make it back to life again. That body of yours without your ego is your enlightened version." The man looked quite puzzled and asked again, "How can my body survive and live without my ego"? The wise man replied, "Your body has the supreme universal intelligence within itself, and your ego is mere stupidity which blocks this intelligence, and your body without your ego will join the unitary movement of life. Then life itself will take care of your body effortlessly."

ANIMAL RIGHTS ON THE CONSTITUTION
Would you mind if your government decides to make a new legislation on your constitution protecting animal rights as seriously as human rights declaration?

SWITCH IN THE MIND
Based on some scientific studies done, most of the animal species do not have a sense of self consciousness in the sense they cannot recognize themselves on the mirror. Of course, they have the physical senses which are part of the consciousness, but they do not have a sense of self awareness. This means they will never know death, and for them there is neither the past nor the future; therefore only a timeless existence in the present. Different from animals,

142

human brain which has the capability to function with an extraordinary level of intelligence do have a self consciousness. So, there is being conscious with the physical senses aware of the reality outside like that of the animals, and there is also the self consciousness which is the feeling of the 'I'. Can the human mind go to the dormant room of being animal like conscious which means a body with fully awakened senses without a feeling of an 'I', and then go to the room of self consciousness only when it is needed? Currently, human mind is in the room of self consciousness almost all the time centered around the 'I'. This creates conflict as a result because there is space of emptiness in the other timeless room which the mind needs desperately for energy. So, can the mind make this switch of going from one room to another whenever necessary so that it can live with more space and therefore with more energy and vitality?

MEDITATIVE QUESTIONING
If the location of your heart and brain can be exchanged with some future technology, would 'you' as the 'ego, persona or self' start dwelling in your heart because it is now located in your skull? Will 'you' then, finally, be looking at this lovely world from the center of your heart? Try to imagine and question this as an actuality, and a deep quality of meditative self awareness should come into being.

FINDING THE DELICATE BALANCE BETWEEN LIVING AND DYING
Whether you are ready or not, some day it will all come to an end. There will be no more sunrises, no minutes, hours or days. All the things you collected, whether treasured or forgotten will pass to someone else. Your wealth, fame and power will be irrelevant. It will not matter what you owned or what you were owed. Your grudges, resentments, frustrations and jealousies will finally disappear. So too, your hopes, ambitions, plans and your do lists will expire. The wins and losses that mattered so much for you will fade away. It won't matter where you came from or what side of the tracks you lived on.
It won't matter whether you were beautiful or brilliant. Even your gender and skin color will be irrelevant. What will matter though is whether you lived with the light of joy and true love. Remembering death sometimes, not as a morbid subject but as an irrevocable fact

of life, will help us to keep rooted in the present moment by reminding us nothing is permanent, and no future is guaranteed. Then enjoyment in the deepening awareness of the present moment becomes the most important thing, and this strong connection with the present through the fact of death will naturally bring a quality of love and joy into our lives.

LET LIFE BE THE DIRECTOR OF YOUR STORY

Why don't we just enjoy being the main actor or the actress of the movie of our own lives and let life be the director? This means surrendering and flowing with the mighty river of life without inward resistance to its swift movements. Seeing the perfect order in the cosmos, and seeing the absolute chaos of humanity; one wonders why humanity does not let this universal intelligence itself be the director of life on earth. We want to be the actor as well as the director, but maybe life itself with its natural intelligence is meant to be the director, and maybe that is the whole meaning of life on earth. And, how can we let life be the director? Isn't the total surrender of the ego an absolute necessity for life to take the seat of the director, and make the movie of your life? Watch the extraordinary love story of the sun, the moon, the stars, and the earth directed by life itself, and then decide whether you or life could be the best director for the filming of your particular story.

A QUOTE

"If you bring forth what is within you, what you bring forth will save you. If you do not bring forth what is within you, what you do not bring forth will destroy you." Jesus

Whatever is in the deeper layers of your consciousness, let it flower to come up to the surface under the light of pure observation. What is within you might not be something likeable such as jealousy, envy, anger, hatred, loneliness, some perverted thoughts etc. Whatever is there deep within you must come to the surface to be observed and understood. And, the only way for this is to give total freedom to that thing to flower and come out. That means no judgment of that thing as being good or bad. Just let it flower without even naming it, and observe it. This also implies being who you actually are rather than having fake masks on your face which veil what is within you. That means one must be totally inwardly naked with no masks of any kind.

How can what is within you be brought forth if there are any masks that will inevitably block it from coming out? So, absolute honesty of being who you actually are with no masks is necessary. If you are trying or pretending to be someone other than who you actually are, then what is within you will be very destructive because it will be imprisoned in the unexposed deeper and darker layers of your consciousness. Also, in your relationships with others, don't keep things inside you. Bring them out, and find a nice way of talking about the things that bother you so that they do not gather in you which is quite a destructive process. So, be direct and genuinely who you actually are, and free what is deep within you to come up to the surface so that it can be clearly seen and exposed with the light of observation. This way of bringing forth what is within you will save you by freeing you.

MOVE AWAY FROM WHAT LOVE IS NOT
Instead of seeking love, be aware and try moving away from what love is not. Move away from environments and people in your life who lack love. Also, move away from what love is not within you; and that is moving away from jealousy, hatred, inward comparison etc. Try it because this very movement away from what love is not might be the only way to love. Instead, we generally want to look for, seek or walk towards love. But, how can we walk towards the unknown which is timeless and anew each moment? We can only walk towards a known destination which means that thing must have its roots in the past, but does love have its roots in time or is love timeless? When we walk towards love, it is the idea of love we have in our time bounded minds that we are walking to. So, this very movement away from what love is not; rather than moving towards love might be the only movement that will take us to the vast ocean of love.

DO WHAT YOU ARE DOING SERIES
DRIVING YOUR CAR
Next time you get in your car for a ride, if you are not in rush, just sit quietly for about a minute after you get into your car. In this time space, just look at the things of your car attentively in silence. Just be aware of the details you probably have never looked at closely before. By doing this, in a subtle way you are opening a new dimension

which is out of the river of time because you have always been starting your car soon after you get in it in order to get to a future destination. Now, you are not in your car just to get to somewhere in future, but you are in it to be aware that you are in a machine called a car in a planet called earth in the vast universe. It would be a miraculous thing for an intelligent creature that has never been to earth to have this experience of driving a car; whereas it has become an ordinary affair for us because time makes us accustomed to it; therefore it curtains the miracle of life which can be perceived only in this present moment. So, stop the flow of time in this 1 minute break of awareness, and then start your car and enjoy the drive. You are now driving your car not to a destination in the future, but you are taking a journey into the now. Your destination is not in the future, but in the now. Be aware that each living moment in your ride is in the now. So your entire journey is in the now, and that means you moved from present to present, and not from the past to a future destination.

GOING DEEPER INTO THE PRESENT

Sometimes, when you are not in rush, get out of the river of time which seems to be flowing from the past into the future, and go deeper into the present instead. Think of your life as a movie for a second; a 60, 70 or 80 years movie. What happens if somehow all the film is burned, except a10 minute distance beginning from now. Then, you would naturally go deeper into the present moment because past and future is vanished. You would then naturally do what you are doing, whatever that thing is, with great attention because you do not have a past anymore to cling to, or a future to project. It might be washing the dishes, ironing, cooking, talking, singing etc. You would be doing what you are doing joyfully because all the film is burned except this 10 minute part. Therefore, there is no past or future to dominate or shadow your relationship with the present. And, the more you burn the film the more you enter into the depths of the present moment. You can burn all the film except 1 week, or 1 minute, or 1 second and go deeper and deeper into the present moment totally moving away from the river of time which flows from the past into the future. The shorter the distance of the film left to live with, the deeper you go into the present moment, and basically there is no limit or end to the unknown depths of the present away from time, and joy of living will meet you there. Burn the film sometimes, and go deeper into the present moment. Of course, what is implied here is burning the film of the psychological memory which makes up the 'me', and not the technical memory with which we need to function properly in daily life.

SOME MEDITATIVE QUESTIONS

Will happiness knock on our door at a certain time as an invited guest while we are expecting and getting prepared for it, or will it come totally unexpectedly anytime?

Should we listen to the sincere critics or just ignore them?

What is not love?

Are you deeply in love with life?

Would you like you if you met you?

Could you post the selfie of your naked soul if it were possible to take a picture of it?

Imagine you could take off your body just like you take off your clothes, and this implies freedom from the identification with the body. When you have time in a quiet place, try to imagine what it would feel like to take off the body. And, what remains after taking off the body?

DO WHAT YOU ARE DOING SERIES
OPENING THE DOOR

When you have some free time with no rush, try opening a door with full presence. Simply, go to a door in your house like the living room or bedroom door, and close the door. Now, first stand next to the door, and look at the door with full natural attention for some time. Look carefully at the qualities of the details of the door like the shape, color…etc. Do it like you have just awakened to life in the vast universe out of nowhere without a past or future, and the first thing you see is this door; similar like a baby looking at something for the first time. Of course it won't be easy, but just do your best. Then, slowly start opening the door like you are opening it for the first time, because as explained, now there is only this door and you in the vast universe with no past and future. This implies that you will open the door with the care of full attention and presence in the 'now' like there is a little baby sleeping behind the door. Do this from time to time, and each time a new quality of attention should come. This might sound strange, but if you really can open the door with total attention in the 'now' totally free from the past and the future, then the quality of attention and the timeless presence in that very act of opening will be the door opening to the light of joyful living.

CONVERSATION WITH THE BELOVED

God said, 'I am life, love life and you will love me. I have given this life to you so that you can make such a love story with life which means with me that all the lovers of heavens will envy your love. That is why you are given this divine life. It will be a race to the top of the mountain of love, not a race to the top of the mountain of the material things, success, fame and money. Don't seek the key to the kingdom of happiness in books, in temples, in mosques, in churches or in rituals as that kingdom lies in the depths of the serene waters of your heart; and there is no way, no key other than such love. You must have such a love story with life, therefore with me as well that all the gods will agree to classify it as the immortal one. You are on earth to create your unique story. And, if you want to know whether your story is good enough then ask yourself this question; "If I were a god, would I classify my life story as an immortal love story with the beloved? You know, lovers must have poems for the beloved to begin with, and then the climb to the mountain tops will begin to get lost in the ecstasy of love."

MEDITATIVE EXERCISE OF LOOKING WITHOUT THE 'EGO'

Hold an item in your hand like a pen, bottle etc. and look at it silently. Be aware that you are making a subtle unconscious division between 'your hand' and 'the item' in the sense of hand being 'yours' as a part of 'your body'; and the item, not a part of your body. So, the eyes look and see 'your' hand, and the 'not your' item. So, the division is about 'yours', and 'not yours'. Can you look in such a way that this division disappears, and there is only 'the' hand holding 'the' item, so that there is unity between your hand and the item? If you try, you will see this will be possible only when there is looking without the 'ego' or the 'observer'; because as long as there is the ego looking, there should be 'ego's' hand holding the 'not ego's' item. If you try you will also realize how difficult it is to end this division because the ego is so very deeply and strongly rooted in us. But, try this meditative exercise from time to time because it will bring a deeper awareness of the ego, and therefore a deeper awareness of living in the present moment because ego is rooted in time, and the very awareness of this is to be present in the 'now'. This is what is meant by the unity in the universe. When there is no ego, then there is unity simply because ego is the very factor of division. You will also feel a subtle sense of peace coming in while you are doing this exercise. It is also great fun. Enjoy!

MEDITATIVE QUESTIONING

If you are told by a doctor 'actually, not theoretically' that you have got exactly 1 year left to live, how would you change your life? Wouldn't you love more? Or, for example, would you be as busy, as angry, as stressful, as hating, as ambitious, as bored, as depressed etc. as you are now? Can you find out what would change in your life with a realistic scenario of having only a year left to live, and can you start applying those changes to your life now? Ask this question **seriously** like it is true and meditate upon it in silence as the answer has great genuine potential to change your life radically in a positive direction.

MEDITATIVE QUESTIONING

Why do humans kill to eat? Eating meat is absolutely not a physical necessity perhaps apart from certain exceptional cases. So, why do humans eat meat? A highly conscious living thing is being killed brutally for that, especially in today's so called modern industrial mass killing. Majority of those who eat meat can't kill an animal themselves because of the violence involved; so they hire somebody else to do the killing. This is the truth whether one likes it or not. So, why do we kill really? If it is not a necessity, then it is for the pleasure of eating meat itself? So are we, the so called highly intelligent human race, killing fellow animals just for the sensual pleasure of eating? If this is so, then don't we make it very difficult for love to knock on the door of our hearts? After all, it would not be an easy task for love to be put up with any kind of brutality.

MEDITATIVE QUESTIONING
Can love, with its joyful light, pay a visit to a heart where any sense of hatred dwells for any reason whatsoever? Can love share the same room with hatred of any kind?

WHICH ONE IS WORSE?
The fear of a possible future event, or the actuality of that event taking place. For example; living with the fear of losing a job, and actually losing the job. Isn't living with the fear of losing a job for days, months or even years worse than the actuality of losing it? Fear of a possible future pain will always imprison us in darkness, because then that fear which has its roots in the future will always keep us away from the light of the "present"; whereas even the pain of the actual thing is taking place in the present. Therefore, light can shine through the actual pain taking place in the present and free us.

So, there is a fundamental difference between the fear of a thing, and that thing actually taking place. With fear, there is eternal darkness. With that thing actually taking place, we might go through certain suffering, but there is light at the end of the tunnel because we stand on the ground of the present moment. So, destroy all psychological fear of possible future events, and get prepared if necessary to actually suffer for those things when they actually take place. In most cases, no suffering will be necessary anyway. Do not fear suffering itself, but do fear psychological fear of suffering.

WHO IS SPIRITUAL?
The one who has practiced methods of meditation or silencing the mind all one's life or the one who truly loved even for a moment of one's life? Is love the factor of opening the spiritual eye, or any kind of spiritual methods prescribed by the latest gurus at a certain price? Can there be a spiritual life without love at the very center?

YOU ARE LIFE
Think of the universe as a giant screen. For an objective outside observer, there is no division of any kind on the screen, but for the

players on the screen there is a division as 'me', and 'not me' which is the rest of the screen. But, the objective truth is that the screen is an inseparable whole, and the source of human conflict originates from the illusion of creating a division as the 'me' and 'not me'. Just like a character in a movie screen saying 'I', but you as the outside observer seeing he is in fact part of the screen of a whole without such division in reality as 'him' being separate from the rest of the screen. When 'me' ends in the mind, then the duality of 'me' and 'not me' ends as well; and at that moment life is perceived through the eyes of that objective outside observer watching the giant screen as a whole. Then, there is no division of 'you' and 'life' anymore, because then you are life itself.

MEDITATIVE QUESTIONING
To be able to live a day like it is one's last day, one must be able to end the attachment to things with one timeless strike in the present moment just like death. Hopefully we will have long lives, but if death comes today are we well prepared to leave the world peacefully? Did we treat our loved ones and friends the way we would if today was our last meeting with them? What would be the quality of the expression in our eyes if those eyes knew they were looking at this beautiful world and human beings for the last time? Can we live this way in our daily lives? If we can't, then what is preventing us?

AWARENESS TEST
Were you aware of the full moon last month?
Are you generally aware of the full moon each month?
Do you take some time to silently watch the full moon?

MEDITATIVE QUESTIONING
Your physical eyes are reading this now, and there is also the 'reader' in this process. Who is that 'reader'? Can you turn inward, and look at that reader 'now'? Can you see the reader clearly? Who is looking at the reader, and is that looker different from the reader? Can the 'reader', the 'looker' and 'you' be one single entity? And if that is so, then the question becomes; "can you look at 'you' now"? But, then isn't it again 'you' trying to look at 'you' which is impossible? Can

there be a quality of looking at you without you? And, can that quality be freedom?

ATTACHMENT TEST
Can you easily take a holiday for a week in a place where internet and mobile phones are not allowed?

MEDITATIVE QUESTIONING
If the electricity is cut off in your area for about 2 hours at night, you will naturally have to be away from Facebook, internet, TV etc. And, if you are lucky enough to have a candle, you will spend this period with your loved ones or alone under the candle light. Would your mind be more in a state of silent meditative peace in this period and why if it would?

AWARENESS TEST
Have you watched something of nature like the sunset, a tree, a flower, a river, the stars or the moon etc. for at least 1 minute in the last 24 hours?

THE CLASS OF SELF KNOWLEDGE
Can you share this on your facebook page?
"My dear friends,

Today is the day for learning about myself through critical awareness as this is the only path to true wisdom. Please tell me very sincerely one thing today that you do not like about me. I demand this from you very sincerely because by doing this you will help me to know myself better. After all, we all have one thing or another that we do not like in our friends and through honest and sincere talks, much healthier relationships can be built up for sure. So, here I am totally open for critics today. Myself or my ego is in the arena to be shot. Go for it, and do not miss the chance! If you aim well with sincerity and shoot with love, then you will hit the target which will take me further in my journey towards wisdom."

WHAT IS THE SELF?
What is the self, the thinker or the observer? Basically, what is this thing called the 'me'? This question itself if pursued deeply and

seriously will take one on the spiritual path of wisdom and realization. The moment this question is put seriously, a shaking awakening will begin taking place in the mind because this question will act as the alarm bell for the sleeper in the mind. With this question, the mind will begin being aware of the sleeper; therefore the sleep itself. This very awareness of the sleep itself will be the awakening process, and going deeper into this question will be the flowering of meditation towards greater inner depths.

AWARENESS TEST
What type and what color were the clothes of the last person you looked at?

PRESENCE TEST
What percentage of your time has been lived totally present in the moment in this last week? Total presence in the moment implies emptiness in the mind with no thought; neither of the future nor of the past.

A) 0-5%   Very low presence
B) 6-20%   Low Presence
C) 21-40%   Medium presence
D) 41-60%   Good presence
E) 61-90 %   Excellent presence
F) 91-99%   Full presence
G) %100   Enlightened presence

MEDITATIVE QUESTIONING
If you were forced to choose from one of the below for the rest of your life which one would you choose?

A) The king or the queen who will run the world

B) A free shepherd or shepherdess who will run the animal world in nature

No kings or queens who will think of changing the world are accepted, as that is the good old trick of the ego. So, the world will stay as it is now, and you can not change it, but you can enjoy all its material richness, fun...etc if you choose to be the king or the queen.

And, remember that you can make a choice once only from the above two options and you are forced to keep that choice for the rest of your life. Which one would you choose then?

A FANTASY QUESTION

If your death would somehow save the world eternally making it into a peaceful heaven forever, what would your reaction be?

A) I would not accept it
B) I would consider it
C) I would not even think for a second and accept it

THE ACTION OF LOVE

You don't send love or pray for a child drowning in the middle of an ocean, do you? You find yourself in the water to save that child without even thinking about it even if your life might be endangered. This is the action of love. Love becomes the absolute master without thought or the ego interfering with such action. In such action, there is no 'me' anymore who will think of his or her life first. True spirituality is all about such action rather than words of love, and one does not need to read any so called spiritual books to jump into the water to save that child taking a risk if necessary. On the contrary, most probably none of the book knowledge about love will help in such a situation, and what good does your spirituality have after reading hundreds of books, meditating for thousands of hours or getting lost in rituals, if you can't act rightly in such a situation. So there is a fundamental difference between the theory and the very actuality of spirituality. Most of the so called spiritual live in the theoretical realm talking endlessly about love whereas only the very few break the chains of the theory and live with the actuality of love. Action of love can never come from a mind which is programmed with the spiritual knowledge of the books, as such action must be totally unconditioned which means free from time as recorded past memory of knowledge.

FIND YOUR SECRET KEY

LITTLE STORIES WITH BIG TRUTHS

by Anonymous

www.facebook.com/FindYourSecretKey

EVERY-MINUTE ZEN

Zen students are with their masters at least two years before they presume to teach others. Nan-in was visited by Tenno, who, having passed his apprenticeship, had become a teacher. The day happened to be rainy, so Tenno wore wooden clogs and carried an umbrella. After greeting him Nan-in remarked: "I suppose you left your wooden clogs in the vestibule. I want to know if your umbrella is on the right or left side of the clogs."

Tenno, confused, had no instant answer. He realized that he was unable to carry his Zen every minute. He became Nan-in's pupil, and he studied six more years to accomplish his every-minute Zen.

Lesson to be learned: Living in the present moment implies giving full attention to what we are doing in the now without a choice. This means there is no such thing as unimportant thing. Every little thing must get attention like it is the most important thing. This can be cooking, cleaning, talking, singing or spending time in toilet. There must the quality of choiceless awareness of whatever we are doing in the present moment. For instance, just before a very important meeting be aware of the quality of the door you walk through. If you walk through that door with no awareness of the door, then you will also not fully be aware of the meeting you will have either. You will not be totally present and calm in the meeting. This is what it means to live totally in the present moment.

TRUST GOD BUT TIE YOUR CAMEL

There was once a man who was on his way back home from market with his camel and, as he'd had a good day, he decided to stop at a mosque along the road and offer his thanks to God. He left his camel outside and went in with his prayer mat and spent several hours offering thanks to Allah, praying and promising that he'd be a good Muslim in the future, help the poor and be an upstanding pillar of his community.

When he emerged it was already dark, and behold – his camel was gone! He immediately flew into a violent temper and shook his fist at the sky, yelling: "You traitor, Allah! How could you do this to me? I put all my trust in you and then you go and stab me in the back like this!"

A passing sufi dervish heard the man yelling and chuckled to himself; "Listen," he said, "Trust God but, you know, tie up your camel."

Lesson to be learned: Never move away from rational intelligence because of so called spirituality. There is a delicate balance between the spiritual intuition and rational intelligence, and to be wise is to walk with such a balance. Love is the perfect balance of spiritual intuition and an extraordinary sense of rational intelligence.

A BUDDHA

In Tokyo in the Meiji era there lived two prominent teachers of opposite characteristics. One, Unsho, an instructor in Shingon, kept Buddha's precepts scrupulously. He never drank intoxicants, nor did he eat after eleven o'clock in the morning. The other teacher, Tanzan, a professor of philosophy at the Imperial University, never observed the precepts. When he felt like eating, he ate, and when he felt like sleeping in the daytime, he slept.

One day Unsho visited Tanzan, who was drinking wine at the time, not even a drop of which is supposed to touch the tongue of a Buddhist.

"Hello, brother," Tanzan greeted him. "Won't you have a drink?"

"I never drink!" exclaimed Unsho solemnly.

"One who does not drink is not even human," said Tanzan.

"Do you mean to call me inhuman just because I do not indulge in intoxicating liquids!" exclaimed Unsho in anger. "Then if I am not human, what am I?"

"A Buddha," answered Tanzan.

Lesson to be learned: Intoxicating liquids are of course not something suggested in a spiritual way of living; as a mind which is free must also be free from the attachment of such drinks. Such a mind which has touched the ultimate joy of living itself will not need any of such liquids anyway, because it will be an ecstatic mind by itself since it has freed itself from all attachment of such things; therefore its bliss will not depend on anything. But, this should not be done by taking a brutal wow of not drinking such liquids. If it is done just because a religion says so, then it merely becomes a restricting rule, and a mind which is restricted this way will never know what the joy of liberation is. How can a mind which is living in the prison of any restriction can ever attain ultimate freedom? It is impossible. But, this does not necessarily mean one will be free to do whatever one desires, or drink as much alcohol as possible; what is needed is intelligent observation of the desire and the dependency of a mind that wants to forget its suffering through such drinks or any other means of escapes. Only such understanding can take one to the path of liberation; certainly not the suppression or the control of any desire because what is suppressed gets stronger and stronger, and freedom can only come through intelligent observation and understanding of 'what is'.

THE HEART DONKEY

There was a man in Turkey who was travelling with his favorite donkey, a faithful companion for years and an animal very close to his heart. At the end of a hard day on the road he came to an inn and decided to rest there for the night. No sooner than he had taken off the saddle bags than a youth working for the inn came out to greet him.

"Salaam Aleikum, sir, welcome to our humble shelter! Please, come inside and get some warm soup and sit beside the fire."

"Of course, I'd love to but first I must make sure my donkey is well cared for." The man said, patting his donkey on the back. The youth smiled generously.

"Please, sir, allow me to attend to such details, you are an honored guest here."

"But it's just that he's an old donkey and needs a nice bed of hay to lie in."

"Sir, we guarantee you the best care possible."

"But you will sweep the floor first to make sure there are no stones? He gets in a terrible mood if he doesn't sleep well."

"Please, sir, just trust me, we are professionals here."

"But you will add some water to his straw – his teeth are getting shakey and he likes just a little fresh grass to begin with."

"Sir, you are embarrassing me!"

"And you will give him a little rubdown along the spine – he goes crazy for that!" "Sir, please just leave everything to me."

So finally the man gave in and entered the establishment to enjoy a fine dinner by the fire and a comfortable bed. Meanwhile the youth rolled his eyes and… then went out to play cards in a nearby den. The man could not sleep somehow, despite the silk sheets, as he kept having nightmares of his donkey chained up without water or food, lying on the cold stone. The vision wouldn't leave him and so he got up in his dressing gown, walked down the steps to the stable and there! His donkey was in exactly the condition he'd imagined – cold, hungry and dying of thirst.

Lesson to be learned: The world is full of those who say whatever is necessary to get their way. When it comes to looking after your heart donkey, it's entirely up to us. We are the only real keepers of our feelings and no one knows better than us what we really need, hence the value of trusting our intuition and taking care of our hearts as though it really were an old, faithful companion.

THE CRITICISM OF MEN

Hodja and his son went on a journey once. Hodja preferred that his son ride the donkey and that he himself go on foot. On the way they met some people who said:

-Look at that healthy young boy! That is today's youth for you. They have no respect for elders. He rides on the donkey and makes his poor father walk!

When they had passed by these people the boy felt very ashamed and insisted that he walk and his father ride the donkey. So Hodja mounted the donkey and the boy walked at his side. A little later they met some other people who said:
-Well, look at that! That poor little boy has to walk while his father rides the donkey.

After they had passed by these people, Hodja told his son:
-The best thing to do is for both of us to walk. Then no one can complain.

So they continued on their journey, both of them walking. A little ways down the road they met some others who said:
-Just take a look at those fools. Both of them are walking under this hot sun and neither of them are riding the donkey!

Hodja turned to his son and said:
-That just goes to show how hard it is to escape the opinions of men.

Lesson to be learned: Do not live your life based on others' opinions, or thinking what the others would say, because society is corrupt. Many people might criticize you on things which most probably they themselves are doing behind the curtain. Most people are hypocrites. So, do not waste your precious life by living it based on this corrupt society's measures. Listen, but find out the truth of things for yourself, and then live with that truth. Do not accept things just because the majority says so. You can be sure that behind the closed doors most of those people do the totally opposite of what they say.

FUR COAT
One day the Hodja was invited to a feast in an important and wealthy family's home. When he arrived, neither the hosts, nor the other guests paid any attention to him. They made him sit at one corner of the table, they didn't ask his opinion on any of the discussed matters, and worst of all, they forgot to pass him the food trays. Nasreddin

Hodja felt left out. Nobody was showing any due respect or offering him food. The servants were passing him by and forgetting to fill his goblet.

A half hour later, the Hodja had enough of being ignored and he quietly slipped out of the house. He went back to his home and changed his clothes. He wore the best and the newest garments he owned. Then, he borrowed a very nice coat with real fur trims from one of his better-off neighbours. With this new attire, he headed back to the house where the banquet was being held.

This time around, everyone noticed the Hodja. The hosts and the servants welcomed him and the other guests treated him with respect. They gave him the best spot at the table and offered him food and drinks. Nasreddin Hodja was very pleased with this new reception. He started to eat with relish and participate in the conversation. However, the guests and the hosts soon noticed that, every now and then, the Hodja was dipping the hem of his coat into his plate and muttering `eat my fur coat, do eat, you eat too.' Everyone was curious.

`Hodja Effendi,' the host finally inquired, `why are you dipping your coat into the food and what is it that you are murmuring?' Nasreddin Hodja was waiting for this opportunity. `I am feeding my coat,' he was glad to explain, `I am telling it to enjoy the food. After all, it is thanks to its fur trims that I am being offered all these delicious treats.'

Note: This is the most famous of all Nasreddin Hodja stories. Its proverbial ending, "ye kurkum, ye!" (eat my fur coat, eat!) is a common phrase in Turkish. It is used to imply the treatment according to the displayed wealth.

Lesson to be learned: The corrupt society measures the value of a human being not by that person's richness in the heart, but by the richness of the pocket. A true friend and a true human being will value another human being only by his or her human qualities, and never by the amount of worldly riches possessed by that human being. Stay away from people who measure the value of a human being by material things. Such people has no love, and they will bring nothing to your life. They will never be there sincerely to help you when you really need them.

K LEARNS NOT TO JUDGE

One day, K was walking his way back home. He did not know what time it was, and he did not want to be late. Unexpectedly, he met devil walking down the street, and he asked for the time, and the devil told K the perfect truth. K asked, "Why?", since K thought devil's business was to pervert the truth; and the devil said, "it was not my intention to do so as I have a broken watch; but by chance, we met at the right time of the day."

K said to himself, "even the devil can speak of absolute truth once in a while, therefore I must never judge anybody. From now on, I will listen to the statement itself, and I will find out for myself the truth or the falseness of the statement. Truth is more important than who says it.

FINAL EXAMINATION

K was having one of the regular morning meditation sessions with his disciples. He was giving a sermon about unconditional love. All of a sudden, the devil came along unexpectedly. He asked for a permission to sit down and join the sermon. K said, 'We do not have the authority to give such permissions about who can join the group. Anybody who is willing to listen can come. We do not choose people; neither do we judge them about their identity.' The devil sat down, and K continued the sermon.

K came to a point in the sermon where he told his disciples that this quality of love must flow like the scent of a flower. He said, 'The flower gives off its scent for any passerby. It cannot choose a particular person who will smell its scent. It is there for all. Love is like this scent of the flower. There is no division as the subject and the object like "I" love "you". There is only love without the object. At this point, the devil asked, 'Does it also include me? Will you teach your disciples to love me as well'? K replied, 'Of course, and your place is quite a special one because you are the final examination to pass in the school of love.' And, all the disciples fell into great laughter. The devil got upset with this answer because he was looking for a confrontation of some kind, and he left harshly.

K said, 'I can never understand this devil, and he will probably never understand the wisdom of love with its simplicity'. And, the disciples started meditating about the final examination.

MEASUREMENT OF THE HUMAN VALUE

K was giving one of his regular morning sermons about the corruption of society, and he told the story of a poor beggar as a metaphor to make it simpler.

The story was about a poor beggar who was begging on the street every day in a little town. He was quite an honest and a very good hearted poor man, but somehow he could not be able to make a living by a proper work. One day, a rich and respectable man of the town was walking down the street where this poor man was begging. When the rich man saw the beggar, he told him a few words in quite an arrogant tone about him being a parasite of society. The poor beggar's heart was terribly broken after hearing such brutal words which he didn't deserve. Then, the poor beggar saw a lottery ticket dropped down right before him on the street. It was probably the ticket of the man who just insulted him viciously. He looked, and he saw the man from a distance. He immediately shouted after the man honestly with no second thoughts of keeping the ticket for himself, but the rich man was quite far away. He did not hear, and walked away. The poor beggar did not know who this man was as he was not a member of the rich and respectable community of the town. The beggar, then, went back home and checked the lottery results from the newspaper, and miraculously he won the big national lottery. He was tremendously happy all day long.

The poor beggar of the down has now become the richest of the town all of a sudden. He soon met the well-respected people of the town as he spent almost all of his money for charity because he had a golden heart. And, in one of the charity events which were sponsored by him, he saw the rich man who insulted him and dropped down the lottery ticket. He immediately went to the man. The rich man did not recognize the beggar since the beggar had a different look now with some proper clothes. The rich man talked to the beggar with great respect and he said, "We are all thankful to god because of having an intelligent and generous person like you as a very respectable member of our society." The same poor beggar who has been insulted as being a parasite of society has now been flattered as the most respectable and intelligent member of the society. The beggar preferred silence because of the terrible ignorance and the empty heart of this man.

After telling the story of the poor beggar, K paused for a while in silence and he said, 'and the terrible irony is that the poor beggar did not even become rich by doing something. He became rich by absolute chance. See how corrupt the society is. The only measurement device used for the valuation of human beings is based on money and success. Whether a human being has a golden heart or not has no importance at all.'

A CUP OF TEA

Nan-in, a Japanese master during the Meiji era (1868-1912), received a university professor who came to inquire about Zen.

Nan-in served tea. He poured his visitor's cup full, and then kept on pouring.

The professor watched the overflow until he no longer could restrain himself. "It is overfull. No more will go in!"

"Like this cup," Nan-in said, "you are full of your own opinions and speculations. How can I show you Zen unless you first empty your cup?"

THE BURDEN

Two monks were returning to the monastery in the evening. It had rained and there were puddles of water on the road sides. At one place a beautiful young woman was standing unable to walk across because of a puddle of water. The elder of the two monks went up to her, lifted her and left her on the other side of the road, and continued his way to the monastery.

In the evening the younger monk came to the elder monk and said, "Sir, as monks, we cannot touch a woman."

The elder monk answered "yes, brother".

Then the younger monk asks again, "but then Sir, how is that you lifted that woman on the roadside ?"

The elder monk smiled at him and told him " I left her on the other side of the road, but you are still carrying her."

FINDING A PIECE OF TRUTH

One day Mara, the Evil One, was travelling through the villages of India with his attendants. he saw a man doing walking meditation whose face was lit up on wonder. The man had just discovered something on the ground in front of him. Mara's attendant asked what that was and Mara replied, "A piece of truth."

"Doesn't this bother you when someone finds a piece of truth, O Evil One?" his attendant asked. "No," Mara replied. "Right after this, they usually make a belief out of it."

MAYBE

Once upon the time there was an old farmer who had worked his crops for many years. One day his horse ran away. Upon hearing the news, his neighbors came to visit. "Such bad luck," they said sympathetically.

"Maybe," the farmer replied.

The next morning the horse returned, bringing with it three other wild horses. "How wonderful," the neighbors exclaimed.

"Maybe," replied the old man.

The following day, his son tried to ride one of the untamed horses, was thrown, and broke his leg. The neighbors again came to offer their sympathy on his misfortune.

"Maybe," answered the farmer.

The day after, military officials came to the village to draft young men into the army. Seeing that the son's leg was broken, they passed him by. The neighbors congratulated the farmer on how well things had turned out.

"Maybe," said the farmer.

CLIFFHANGER

One day while walking through the wilderness a man stumbled upon a vicious tiger. He ran but soon came to the edge of a high cliff. Desperate to save himself, he climbed down a vine and dangled over the fatal precipice.

As he hung there, two mice appeared from a hole in the cliff and began gnawing on the vine.

Suddenly, he noticed on the vine a plump wild strawberry. He plucked it and popped it in his mouth. It was incredibly delicious!

Lesson to be learned: Live and enjoy the present moment totally free from the past and future.

THE BLIND MEN AND THE ELEPHANT

Several citizens ran into a hot argument about God and different religions, and each one could not agree to a common answer. So they came to the Lord Buddha to find out what exactly God looks like.

The Buddha asked his disciples to get a large magnificent elephant and four blind men. He then brought the four blind to the elephant and told them to find out what the elephant would "look" like.

The first blind men touched the elephant leg and reported that it "looked" like a pillar. The second blind man touched the elephant tummy and said that an elephant was a wall. The third blind man touched the elephant ear and said that it was a piece of cloth. The fourth blind man hold on to the tail and described the elephant as a piece of rope. And all of them ran into a hot argument about the "appearance" of an elephant.

The Buddha asked the citizens: "Each blind man had touched the elephant but each of them gives a different description of the animal. Which answer is right?"

Lesson to be learned: The idea, knowledge or the belief of god is never the real thing itself. They make one rather blind. One must first die to all beliefs, ideas and knowledge about god or truth to be able to start seeking the truth.

RIGHT AND WRONG

When Bankei held his seclusion-weeks of meditation, pupils from many parts of Japan came to attend. During one of these gatherings a pupil was caught stealing. The matter was reported to Bankei with the request that the culprit be expelled. Bankei ignored the case.

Later the pupil was caught in a similar act, and again Bankei disregarded the matter. This angered the other pupils, who drew up a petition asking for the dismissal of the thief, stating that otherwise they would leave in a body.

When Bankei had read the petition he called everyone before him. "You are wise brothers," he told them. "You know what is right and what is not right. You may go somewhere else to study if you wish, but this poor brother does not even know right from wrong. Who will teach him if I do not? I am going to keep him here even if all the rest of you leave." A torrent of tears cleansed the face of the brother who had stolen. All desire to steal had vanished.

Lesson to be learned: Those who are on the false path are the ones who need unconditional love the most.

THE MOON CANNOT BE STOLEN

Ryokan, a Zen master, lived the simplest kind of life in a little hut at the foot of a mountain. One evening a thief visited the hut only to discover there was nothing in it to steal.

Ryokan returned and caught him. "You may have come a long way to visit me," he told the prowler, "and you should not return empty-handed. Please take my clothes as a gift."

The thief was bewildered. He took the clothes and slunk away.

Ryokan sat naked, watching the moon. "Poor fellow, " he mused, "I wish I could give him this beautiful moon."

Lesson to be learned: The only true wealth is the richness of the heart which can perceive the beauty of the world rather than the material things the world can offer.

THE GATES OF PARADISE

A soldier named Nobushige came to Hakuin, and asked: "Is there really a paradise and a hell?"

"Who are you?" inquired Hakuin.

"I am a samurai," the warrior replied.

"You, a soldier!" exclaimed Hakuin. "What kind of ruler would have you as his guard? Your face looks like that of a beggar."

Nobushige became so angry that he began to draw his sword, but Hakuin continued: "So you have a sword! Your weapon is probably much too dull to cut off my head."

As Nobushige drew his sword Hakuin remarked: "Here open the gates of hell!"

At these words the samurai, perceiving the master's discipline, sheathed his sword and bowed.

"Here open the gates of paradise," said Hakuin.

Lesson to be learned: We create our own hell and heaven in this world. Peace, love and joy is the entrance of paradise in this world.

THE STORY OF A BLIND GIRL

There was a blind girl who hated herself just because she was blind. She hated everyone, except her loving boyfriend. He was always there for her. She said that if she could only see the world, she would marry her boyfriend.

One day, someone donated a pair of eyes to her and then she could see everything, including her boyfriend. Her boyfriend asked her, "now that you can see the world, will you marry me?"

The girl was shocked when she saw that her boyfriend was blind too, and refused to marry him. Her boyfriend walked away in tears, and later wrote a letter to her saying: "Just take care of my eyes dear."

THE SECRET OF HAPPINESS

A son of shopkeeper was sent to the wisest man in the World to learn the secret of happiness. The wise man lived on a beautiful castle high atop a mountain. To reach there the lad had to go through the desert for 40 days.

The lad on entering the main room of the castle, saw a hive of activity: tradesmen came and went, people were conversing in the corners, a small orchestra was playing soft music, and there was a table covered with platters of the most delicious food. The wise man conversed with everyone, and the boy had to wait for two hours before it was his turn to get his attention.

The wise man listened attentively and then suggested that the boy look around the palace and return in two hours to get the explanation.

"Meanwhile, I want to ask you to do something", said the wise man, handing the boy a teaspoon that held two drops of oil. "As you wander around, carry this spoon with you without allowing the oil to spill".

The boy began climbing and descending the many stairways of the palace, keeping his eyes fixed on the spoon. After two hours, he returned to the room where the wise man was. "Well", asked the wise man, "Did you see the Persian tapestries that are hanging in my dining hall? Did you see the garden that it took the master gardener ten years to create? Did you notice the beautiful parchments in my library?"

The boy was embarrassed to confess that he had observed nothing. His only concern had been not to spill the oil that was entrusted to him.

"Then go back and observe the marvels of my world", ordered the wise man.

Relieved, the boy picked up the spoon and returned to his exploration of the palace, this time observing all of the works of art on the ceilings and the walls. He saw the gardens, the mountains all around him, the beauty of the flowers, and the taste with which everything had been selected. Upon returning to the wise man, he related in detail everything he had seen.

"But where are the drops of oil I entrusted to you?" asked the wise man. Looking down at the spoon he held, the boy saw that the oil was gone.

Said the wise man ,"The secret of happiness is to see all the marvels of the world and never to forget the drops of oil on the spoon".

Lesson to be learned: Happiness can not be found on a direction which we choose to look at. We should choicelessly be aware of life as a whole rather than looking for happiness in one particular direction. For example, One decides to follow a so called spiritual path, and one only sees that path and nothing else, or one decides to be a successful business man in order to be happy and totally forgets the rest of life as a whole. So, happiness can not be found on any certain particular direction, and we must look at the picture of life as a whole. We will naturally focus on certain things for various reasons, but while focusing on such things we must never lose our connection with the totality of life. If we do, then we get lost in a small part of life, hence joy which is life itself as a whole moves away in a very subtle way.

THE STORY OF A WOODCUTTER

Once upon a time, a very strong woodcutter asked for a job in a timber merchant and he got it. The pay was really good and so was the work condition. For those reasons, the woodcutter was determined to do his best. His boss gave him an axe and showed him the area where he supposed to work.

The first day, the woodcutter brought 18 trees.

"Congratulations," the boss said. "Go on that way!"

Very motivated by the boss' words, the woodcutter tried harder the next day, but he could only bring 15 trees. The third day he tried even harder, but he could only bring 10 trees. Day after day he was bringing less and less trees.

"I must be losing my strength", the woodcutter thought. He went to the boss and apologized, saying that he could not understand what was going on.

"When was the last time you sharpened your axe?" the boss asked.

"Sharpen? I had no time to sharpen my axe. I have been very busy trying to cut trees…"

Lesson to be learned: Do not be concerned with the end result when you are doing something, because if you do, then you are not doing the thing with natural full attention in the present moment since that end result is in time, and it prevents you giving full attention in the "now". When you are not concerned with the end, then you are doing the thing in the present moment totally just for the love of it. Therefore you see things very clearly; whereas you will be blinded with the end result. Out of such very doing itself in the present moment with its natural attention, whatever is being done will be done perfectly and beautifully.

ARE YOU AN EAGLE OR A CHICKEN?

Once upon a time, at a large mountainside there was an eagle nest with 4 large eagle eggs inside.

One day, an earthquake rocked the mountain causing one of the eggs to roll down to a chicken farm, located in the valley below.

The chickens knew that they must protect the eagle egg. Eventually, the eagle egg hatched and a beautiful eagle was born.

Being chickens, the chickens raised the eagle to be a chicken. The eagle loved his home and family but it seemed his spirit cried out for more.

One day, the eagle looked to the skies above and noticed a group of mighty eagles soaring. "Oh," the eagle cried, "I wish I could soar like those birds."

The chickens roared with laughter, "You cannot soar like those. You are a chicken and chickens do not soar." The eagle continued staring at his real family up above, dreaming that he could be like them.

Each time the eagle talked about his dreams, he was told it couldn't be done.

That was what the eagle learned to believe. After time, the eagle stopped dreaming and continued to live his life as a chicken.

Finally, after a long life as a chicken, the eagle passed away.

Lesson to be learned: The conditioned mind is limited, and until it is free from all conditioning it can never discover its full potential, and also it can never see the truth. What it will see is only its limited conditioning. You become what you believe, and if you listen to the words of chickens, then you will never discover the free flight of the eagle within yourself.

ANGER, ENVY & INSULTS
Near Tokyo lived a great Samurai, now old, who decided to teach Zen Buddhism to young people.

One afternoon, a warrior – known for his complete lack of scruples – arrived there. The young and impatient warrior had never lost a fight.

Hearing of the Samurai's reputation, he had come to defeat him, and increase his fame.

All the students were against the idea, but the old man accepted the challenge.

All gathered on the town square, and the young man started insulting the old master. He threw a few rocks in his direction, spat in his face, shouted every insult under the sun – he even insulted his ancestors.

For hours, he did everything to provoke him, but the old man remained impassive. At the end of the afternoon, by now feeling exhausted and humiliated, the impetuous warrior left.

Disappointed by the fact that the master had received so many insults and provocations, the students asked: "How could you bear such indignity? Why didn't you use your sword, even knowing you might lose the fight, instead of displaying your cowardice in front of us all?"

"If someone comes to you with a gift, and you do not accept it, who does the gift belong to?" – asked the old Samurai.

"He who tried to deliver it." – replied one of his disciples.

"The same goes for envy, anger and insults." – said the master. "When they are not accepted, they continue to belong to the one who carried them."

Lesson to be learned: Be neutrally silent with the ignorant like a wise book, and the ignorant will be talking to a mirror of his own.

THE PEACEFUL MIND

There once was a farmer who discovered that he had lost his watch in the barn. It was no ordinary watch because it had sentimental value for him.

After searching high and low among the hay for a long while; he gave up and enlisted the help of a group of children playing outside the barn.

He promised them that the person who found it would be rewarded.

Hearing this, the children hurried inside the barn, went through and around the entire stack of hay but still could not find the watch. Just when the farmer was about to give up looking for his watch, a little boy went up to him and asked to be given another chance.

The farmer looked at him and thought, "Why not? After all, this kid looks sincere enough."

So the farmer sent the little boy back in the barn. After a while the little boy came out with the watch in his hand! The farmer was both happy and surprised and so he asked the boy how he succeeded where the rest had failed.

The boy replied, "I did nothing but sit on the ground and listen. In the silence, I heard the ticking of the watch and just looked for it in that direction."

Lesson to be learned: A peaceful mind is more sensitive and perceptive than a mind which is lost in the noise of its own. Allow a few minutes of silence to enter into your mind every day especially in the morning, and see how sharply it helps you to set your life the way you expect it to be. You might also experience this in different ways in your daily life. You look for something crazily and you find the thing only when you give up, or you desire something so much and do all kinds of things, but the thing comes to you easily and effortlessly only when you stop doing anything. The natural order of the universe comes into our lives only through the silence of a peaceful mind, and then we begin seeing things very clearly and act intelligently. Without that peace with its silence, we are like the blind living in the wonder land.

THE EVIL YOU DO REMAINS WITH YOU

A woman baked chapatti (roti) for members of her family and an extra one for a hungry passerby. She kept the extra chapatti on the window sill, for whosoever would take it away. Every day, a beggar came and took away the chapatti. He would express no gratitude but would muttered: "The evil you do remains with you: The good you do, comes back to you!" This went on, day after day. Every day, he came, picked up the chapatti and uttered the words: "The evil you do, remains with you: The good you do, comes back to you!" The woman felt irritated. "Not a word of gratitude," she said to herself... "Everyday this beggar utters this jingle! What does he mean?" she said. One day, exasperated, she decided to get rid of him forever" She added poison to the chapatti she prepared for him!

As she was about to keep it on the window sill, her hands trembled. She realized her terrible mistake ."What is this I am doing?" she said. She threw the chapatti into the fire, prepared another one and kept it on the window sill. As usual, the beggar came, picked up the chapatti and muttered his daily words: "The evil you do, remains with you: The good you do, comes back to you!"

The beggar proceeded on his way, blissfully unaware of what had happened. Every day, as the woman placed the chapatti on the window sill, she offered a prayer for her son who had gone to a distant place to seek his fortune. For many months, she had no news of him.

That very evening, there was a knock on the door. As she opened it, she was surprised to find her son standing in the doorway. He had grown thin and lean. His garments were tattered and torn. He was hungry, starved and weak. As he saw his mother, he said, "Mom, it's a miracle I'm here. While I was but a mile away, I felt so weak that I collapsed. I would have died, but just then an old beggar passed by. I begged of him for some food, and he was kind enough to give me a whole chapatti. As he gave it to me, he said, "This is what I eat everyday: today, I shall give it to you, for your need is greater than mine!"

Hearing these words, the mother's face turned pale. She leaned against the door for support. She remembered the poisoned chapatti that she had made that morning. Had she not burnt it in the fire, it would have been eaten by her own son, and he would have lost his life!

It was then that she realized the significance of the words: "The evil you do remains with you."

Lesson to be learned: Doing evil to others is doing evil to ourselves, and doing good to others is doing good to ourselves.

THE CRACKED POT

A water bearer in India had two large pots, each hung on each end of a pole which he carried across his neck. One of the pots had a crack in it, and while the other pot was perfect and always delivered a full portion of water at the end of the long walk from the stream to the master's house, the cracked pot arrived only half full.

For a full two years this went on daily, with the bearer delivering only one and a half pots full of water in his master's house. Of course, the perfect pot was proud of its accomplishments.

But the poor cracked pot was ashamed of its own imperfection, and miserable that it was able to accomplish only half of what it had been made to do. After two years of what it perceived to be a bitter failure, it spoke to the water bearer one day by the stream.

"I am ashamed of myself, and I want to apologize to you."

"Why?" asked the bearer. "What are you ashamed of?"

"I have been able to deliver only half my load because this crack in my side causes water to leak out all the way back to your master's house. Because of my flaws, you have to do all of this work, and you don't get full value from your efforts," the pot said.

The water bearer felt sorry for the old cracked pot, and in his compassion he said, "As we return to the master's house, I want you to specially notice the beautiful flowers along the path."

Indeed, as they went up the hill, the old cracked pot noticed the sun warming the beautiful wild flowers on the side of the path. But at the end of the trail, it still felt bad because it had leaked out half its load, and so again the pot apologized to the bearer for its failure.

The bearer said to the pot, "Did you notice that there were flowers only on your side of your path, but not on the other pot's side? That's because I have taken advantage of your flaw . I planted flower seeds on your side of the path, and every day while we walk back from the stream, you've watered them. For two years I have been able to pick these beautiful flowers to decorate my master's table. Without you being just the way you are and without your help, he would not have this beauty to grace his house."

Lesson to be learned: Do not underestimate yourself by comparing yourself with others. It's our differences that make us unique and beautiful, and only by true wisdom our uniqueness will find the natural ground to flower.

THE WORLD FROM THE EYES OF INNOCENCE

One day a father of a very wealthy family took his son on a trip to the country with the firm purpose of showing his son how poor people can be. They spent a couple of days and nights on the farm of what would be considered a very poor family. On their return from their trip, the father asked his son, "How was the trip?" "It was great, Dad." "Did you see how poor people can be?" the father asked. "Oh Yeah" said the son. "So what did you learn from the trip?" asked the father. The son answered, "I saw that we have one dog and they had four. We have a pool that reaches to the middle of our garden and they have a creek that has no end. We have imported lanterns in our garden and they have the stars at night. Our patio reaches to the front yard and they have the whole horizon. We have a small piece of land to live on and they have fields that go beyond our sight. We have servants who serve us, but they serve others. We buy our food, but they grow theirs. We have walls around our property to protect us, they have friends to protect them." With this the boy's father was speechless. Then his son added, "Thanks dad for showing me how poor we are."

Lesson to be learned: Heavens can be seen only when the eyes are made innocent like that of a child's. No amount of money can buy a single moment of joy as it is for free. This world is all about how we perceive it. Like in above story, what is possibly seen as hell for the adults can be seen as heaven through the eyes of a child whose mind is not corrupted and conditioned by the society that worships so much to the material things of the world. Truth is so simple to be seen when the eyes, hearts and minds are made innocent. Then heavens become visible right here, right now, in this world.

PRINCESS HILDE OF THE KINGDOM OF HAPPINESS

Once upon a time there was a kingdom with an ancient prophecy that spoke of a Princess without a palace. The prophecy said that as soon as that Princess found her palace, she would be the wisest and fairest Queen there had ever been. That kingdom had a royal family who had lived in a beautiful palace for generations. But there was a great earthquake which destroyed the palace and killed the King and Queen. Their two daughters, Princess Nora and Princess Hilde, managed to survive. After this tragedy, Nora understood that she, being the elder sister, might be the Princess mentioned in the prophecy. Accompanied by her sister, Nora devoted herself to finding her new palace. During their travels they met a wise old man who gave them an old key that would open the palace doors.

"I have no idea where the palace will be", said the old man, "All I know is that you should try this key wherever you seek it".

And Nora went with her sister, trying the key on all the palace doors they found. When there were no more palaces to try, they thought maybe the palace would just be some large important house, but neither did the key fit any of those. Fed up, the sisters lost hope of ever finding their palace. They had spent so much time away, travelling and searching, that no one now missed them. Neither did they have any money or jewels left, and when they arrived at a poor village they had to work in the fields alongside all the poor people who, not knowing that the sisters were royalty, took them in as though they were two homeless orphans.

The sisters lived there for some years. They worked hard, and knew what hunger was, and how life could be so difficult, but people loved them so much that they came to be very happy, and they gradually forgot their royal past. One night, while tidying Nora's things, Hilde found the old key. Amused, she took it to her sister, and they reminisced about their search for their own magnificent palace.

"There still must be some palace, hidden in some little forest, just waiting for us to find it," said Nora, with a glimmer of hope.

"Well, you know what I think," answered her younger sister, "that I don't need anything else to be happy. We spent months travelling from castle to castle to live the life of Queens, but I have never been so happy as I am now, even though we don't have much. If I had to choose a palace," she continued, joyfully dancing about by the door, "it would be this little cabin." she ended, laughing, and then with a solemn gesture placing the key in the cabin door.

Just then, the room filled with lights and music, and from that old door arose a wonderful palace filled with life and colour. The place became totally transformed; there were fountains, gardens, and animals. The village people marvelled at all of this. The only thing which remained as it had been was the cabin door, reminding everyone of how Hilde the Wonderful – which was what they called their wise Queen – had found that in a simple, humble life lay the doorway to happiness, not only for herself, but for all the inhabitants of that land.

Lesson to be learned: The door to the Kingdom of Happiness is not to be found in the flamboyant and sophisticated things in life, but rather in the right, simple and humble way of approaching life.

TRUE LOVE

Husband comes home drunk and breaks some crockery, vomits and falls down on the floor... Wife pulls him up and cleans everything. Next day when he gets up he expects her to be really angry with him.... He prays that they should not have a fight...

He finds a note near the table... "Honey..your favorite breakfast is ready on the table, I had to leave early to buy grocery... I'll come running back to you, my love. I love you. ..."

He gets surprised and asks his son.., 'what happened last night..?' Son told: "When mom pulled you to bed and tried removing your boots and shirt. You were dead drunk and you said: Hey Lady ! Leave Me Alone…I am Married !!!"

Lesson to be learned: Always stay loyal to those who love you.

TEARS OF LOVE

From the very beginning, girl's family objected strongly on her dating this guy, saying that it has got to do with family background, and that the girl will have to suffer for the rest of her life if she were to be with him. Due to family's pressure, the couple quarreled very often. Though the girl loved the guy deeply, she always asked him: "How deep is your love for me?" As the guy is not good with his words, this often caused the girl to be very upset. With that and the family's pressure, the girl often vents her anger on him. As for him, he only endured it in silence.

After a couple of years, the guy finally graduated & decided to further his studies overseas. Before leaving, he proposed to the girl: "I'm not very good with words. But all I know is that I love you. If you allow me, I will take care of you for the rest of my life. As for your family, I'll try my best to talk them round. Will you marry me?" The girl agreed, and with the guy's determination, the family finally gave in and agreed to let them get married. So before he left, they got engaged. The girl went out to the working society, whereas the guy was overseas, continuing his studies. They sent their love through letters and phone calls. Though it was hard, but both never thought of giving up.

One day, while the girl was on her way to work, she was knocked down by a car that lost control. When she woke up, she saw her parents beside her bed. She realized that she was badly injured. Seeing her mum cry, she wanted to comfort her. But she realized that all that could come out of her mouth was just a sigh. She had lost her voice. The doctor says that the impact on her brain has caused her to lose her voice. Listening to her parents' comfort, but with nothing coming out from her, she broke down. Only silent cry accompanied her during her stay in the hospital.

Upon reaching home, everything seems to be the same. Except for the ringing tone of the phone which pierced into her heart every time it rang. She does not wish to let the guy know and not wanting to be a burden to him, she wrote a letter to him saying that she does not wish to wait any longer. With that, she sent the ring back to him. In return, the guy sent millions and millions of reply and countless phone calls. All the girl could do besides crying was still crying. The parents decided to move away, hoping that she could eventually forget everything and be happy. With a new environment, the girl learnt sign language and started a new life. Telling herself everyday that she must forget the guy.

One day, her friend came and told her that he's back. She asked her friend not to let him know what happened to her. Since then, there wasn't any more news of him. A year has passed and her friend came with an envelope, containing an invitation card for the guy's wedding. The girl was shattered. When she opened the letter, she saw her name on it instead. When she was about to ask her friend what was going on, she saw the guy standing in front of her. He used sign language to tell her, "I've spent a year to learn sign language. Just to let you know that I've not forgotten our promise. Let me have the chance to be your voice. I Love You." With that, he slipped the ring back into her finger. She felt a sense of great peace with divine tears of love coming from her eyes.

Lesson to be learned: There are no barriers if one truly loves, and one will do anything to be with the beloved.

SHE GAVE ALL HER HEART

A boy and a girl were playing together. The boy had a collection of marbles. The girl had some sweets with her. The boy told the girl that he will give her all his marbles in exchange for her sweets. The girl agreed. The boy kept the biggest and the most beautiful marble aside and gave the rest to the girl. The girl gave him all her sweets as she had promised.

That night, the girl slept peacefully. But the boy couldn't sleep as he kept wondering if the girl had hidden some sweets from him the way he had hidden his best marble.

Lesson to be learned: The only true love is unconditional, and in that, one gives hundred percent of one's heart. Even ninety-nine percent is not good enough, because even the remaining very small fraction will be the 'condition' which will deny the 'unconditional'. If you don't give your hundred percent in a relationship, you'll always keep doubting if the other person has given his or her hundred percent. This is applicable for any relationship like love, employer-employee, friendship relationship etc. Give your hundred percent to everything you do and sleep peaceful in the bed of wisdom when the night comes.

THE ECHO OF LIFE

A son and his father were walking in the mountains. Suddenly, his son fell, hurt himself and screamed: "AAAhhhhhhhhhhh!!!" To his surprise, he heard the voice repeating, somewhere in the mountain: "AAAhhhhhhhhhhh!!!" Curious, he yelled: "Who are you?" He received the answer: "Who are you?" Angered at the response, he screamed: "Coward!" He received the answer: "Coward!" He looked to his father and asked: "What's going on?"

The father smiled and said: "My son, pay attention." And then he screamed to the mountain: "I admire you!" The voice answered: "I admire you!" Again the father screamed: "You are a champion!" The voice answered: "You are a champion!" The boy was surprised and confused. Then the father explained: "People call this echo, but really this is Life."

Lesson to be learned: Life out there is a mirror reflection of what we are inwardly, and if we change inwardly then our outward reality of life which is the reflection of the inner changes as a natural consequence.

WHAT DO CHILDREN REALLY NEED?

A man came home from work late, tired and irritated, to find his five year old son waiting for him at the door.

SON: "Daddy, may I ask you a question?"
DAD: "Yeah sure, what is it?" replied the man.
SON: "Daddy, how much do you make an hour?"
DAD: "That's none of your business. Why do you ask such a thing?" the man said angrily.
SON: "I just want to know. Please tell me, how much do you make an hour?"
DAD: "If you must know, I make 10 Dollars an hour."
SON: "Oh," the little boy replied, with his head down.
SON: "Daddy, may I please borrow 5 Dollars?"

The father was furious, "If the only reason you asked that is so you can borrow some money to buy a silly toy or some other nonsense, then go straight to your room. I can't spend dollars for silly things."

After the man had calmed down, and started to think; maybe he was harsh on the boy since he rarely asked for money. He went to little boy's room and asked; "Are you asleep, son?" "No daddy, I'm awake," replied the boy. "I've been thinking, maybe I was too hard on you earlier" said the man, "Here's the 5 Dollars you asked for." The little boy sat up, smiling. "Oh, thank you daddy!" He yelled. Then, reaching under his pillow he pulled out some crumpled up bills. The man realized that the boy already had money, started to get angry again. The little boy slowly counted out his money, and then looked up at his father. "Why do you want more money if you already have some?" the father shouted." Because I didn't have enough, but now I do" the little boy replied. "Daddy, I have 10 Dollars now. Can I buy an hour of your time? Please come home early tomorrow. I would like to have dinner with you."

Lesson to be learned: It is an unfortunate fact that in today's ruthless world many have to work a lot to make a living, and that might naturally cause them to spend less time with their children. But, no matter what, make sure you spend enough time with your children by trying your best, because what children really need most, more than toys, expensive clothes or education etc, more than anything basically; is some love from the parents, and that demands some time to be spent with them. Children will be unhealthy even if they get all the expensive material things of the highest quality if they can't get true love and attention from their parents, and they will be very healthy even if the parents are poor and can not offer much but this true love.

EFFORTLESS PEACE

Once Buddha was walking from town to town with his followers. This was in the initial days. They happened to pass a lake and Buddha told one of his disciples, "I am thirsty. Get me some water from that lake."

The disciple walked up to the lake and noticed that some people were washing clothes in the water and he also saw a bullock cart crossing through the lake. As a result, the water became very muddy, very turbid. The disciple returned to tell Buddha; "The water in there is very muddy. I don't think it is fit to drink."

After about half an hour, again Buddha asked the same disciple to go back to the lake and get him the water to drink. The disciple obediently went back to the lake. This time he found that the lake had absolutely clear water in it. The mud had settled down and the water above it looked fit to be had. So he collected some water in a pot and brought it to Buddha.

Buddha looked at the water, and then he looked up at the disciple and said, "See what you did to make the water clean. You let it be and the mud settled down on its own and you got clear water. Your mind is also like that. When it is disturbed, just let it be. Give it a little time. It will settle down on its own. You don't have to put in any effort to calm it down. It will happen effortlessly."

Lesson to be learned: Peace of mind can come only with a quality of effortlessness inwardly. The very effort to reach a peaceful state implies conflict; therefore it denies peace. Peace will come effortlessly when there is a deep understanding of the ways of the mind which creates perpetual conflict. The total surrendering of the ego will be the birth of this effortless state of the mind, as the very nature of the ego is conflict.

SUSPENDED COFFEE

We entered a little coffee house with a friend of mine and gave our order. While we were approaching our table two people came in and went to the counter:

'Five coffees, please. Two of them for us and three suspended'

They paid for their order, took the two and left . I asked my friend:

'What are those 'suspended' coffees ?'

'Wait for it and you will see.'

More people entered. Two girls asked for one coffee each, paid and left . The next order was for seven coffees and it was made by three lawyers – three for them and four 'suspended'. While I still wondered what was the deal with those 'suspended' coffees I enjoyed the sunny weather and the beautiful view towards the square in front of the café.

Suddenly a man dressed in shabby clothes who looked like a beggar came in through the door and kindly asked, 'Do you have a suspended coffee ?'

It's simple: people paid in advance for a coffee meant for someone who could not afford a warm beverage.

The tradition with the suspended coffees started in Naples, but it has spread all over the world and in some places you can order not only a suspended coffee, but also a sandwich or a whole meal."

Lesson to be learned: Always try your best to preserve the traditions that support the ones in need.

THE GARBAGE TRUCK

One day I hopped in a taxi and we took off for the airport.

We were driving in the right lane when suddenly a black car jumped out of a parking space right in front of us.

My taxi driver slammed on his brakes, skidded, and missed the other car by just inches!

The driver of the other car whipped his head around and started yelling at us!

My taxi driver just smiled and waved at the guy. And I mean, really friendly.

So I asked, "Why did you just do that? This guy almost ruined your car and sent us to the hospital!"

This is when my taxi driver taught me what I now call, "The Law of the Garbage Truck."

He explained that many people are like garbage trucks. They run around full of garbage(frustration, anger, and disappointment, etc.). As their garbage piles up, they need a place to dump it and sometimes they'll dump it on you. Don't take it personally. Just smile, wave, wish them well, and move on. Don't take their garbage and spread it to other people at work, at home, or on the streets. Life is ten percent what you make it and ninety percent how you take it!

Lesson to be learned: Don't take things personally all the time. In today's stressful world, people can easily get angry, but that does not necessarily mean we are the enemy target. What should we do if we face such an occasion? Should we respond with anger as well and waste our precious life energy, or should we just wisely and quietly move on knowing these poor people are so very stressed? If we respond with anger, then we also fall into the trap of ignorance with the other, but with love we continue on our path of wisdom, perhaps helping the other also with such love to get out of the trap of ignorance.

WHO RULES THE WORLD

"Who rules the world? Is it the rich and the powerful?" asked the pupil. "You rule it." replied the master calmly; "Your ego, in essence, is no different from those rich and powerful. You are just like them in your greed, ambition to have more, desire to dominate others; therefore true revolution is not against the system out there, but it is against the system in your own mind."

BEING A DISCIPLE OF JESUS

Pastor Jeremiah transformed himself into a homeless person and went to the 10,000 member church that he was to be introduced as the head pastor at that morning.

He walked around his soon to be church for 30 minutes while it was filling with people for service, only 3 people out of the 10,000 people said hello to him. He asked people for change to buy food but no one in the church gave him change. He went into the sanctuary to sit down in the front of the church and was asked by the ushers if he would please sit in the back. He greeted people to be greeted back with stares and dirty looks, with people looking down on him and judging him. As he sat in the back of the church, he listened to the church announcements and such. When all that was done, the elders went up and were excited to introduce the new pastor of the church to the congregation. "We would like to introduce to you Pastor Jeremiah." The congregation looked around clapping with joy and anticipation.

The homeless man sitting in the back stood up and started walking down the aisle. The clapping stopped with all eyes on him. He walked up the altar and took the microphone from the elders (who were in on this) and paused for a moment, then he recited:

"Then the King will say to those on his right, 'Come, you who are blessed by my Father; take your inheritance, the kingdom prepared for you since the creation of the world."

"For I was hungry and you gave me something to eat, I was thirsty and you gave me something to drink, I was a stranger and you invited me in, I needed clothes and you clothed me, I was sick and you looked after me, I was in prison and you came to visit me."

Then the righteous will answer him, "Lord, when did we see you hungry and feed you, or thirsty and give you something to drink?

When did we see you a stranger and invite you in, or needing clothes and clothe you? When did we see you sick or in prison and go to visit you?"

The King will reply, "Truly I tell you, whatever you did for one of the least of these brothers and sisters of mine, you did for me."

After he recited this, he looked towards the congregation and told them all what he had experienced that morning. Many began to cry and many heads were bowed in shame.

He then said, "Today I see a gathering of people, not a church of Jesus. The world has enough people, but not enough disciples. When will you decide to become disciples?"

Lesson to be learned: Unconditional love which must be the very essence of a truly spiritual life is a serious matter rather than a kind of entertainment and money making business like most of the so called new age spirituality of today. Such love of the unconditional kind does not exclude any human being including the homeless ones; and perhaps especially such terribly suffering souls who are the most unfortunate outcome of human confusion, greed and lack of love.

FIND YOUR SECRET KEY

ENLIGHTENING QUOTES
Selected by Memo Ozdogan

www.facebook.com/FindYourSecretKey

"Happiness is strange; it comes when you are not seeking it. When you are not making an effort to be happy, then unexpectedly, mysteriously, happiness is there, born of purity, of a loveliness of being."
Jiddu Krishnamurti

"There is no end to education. It is not that you read a book, pass an examination, and finish with education. The whole of life, from the moment you are born to the moment you die, is a process of learning."
Jiddu Krishnamurti

"You cannot reconcile creativeness with technical achievement. You may be perfect in playing the piano, and not be creative. You may be able to handle color, to put paint on canvas most cleverly, and not be a creative painter...having lost the song, we pursue the singer. We learn from the singer the technique of song, but there is no song; and I say the song is essential, the joy of singing is essential. When the joy is there, the technique can be built up from nothing; you will invent your own technique, you won't have to study elocution or style. When you have, you see, and the very seeing of beauty is an art."
Jiddu Krishnamurti

"If you love, not god, that's very easy to love god because it is an abstraction, it has not much meaning, but if you love, that very love is god, that very love is sacred."
Jiddu Krishnamurti

"You cannot live without dying. You cannot live if you do not die psychologically every minute. This is not an intellectual paradox. To live completely, wholly, every day as if it were a new loveliness, there must be dying to everything of yesterday, otherwise you live mechanically, and a mechanical mind can never know what love is or what freedom is."
Jiddu Krishnamurti

"You must understand the whole of life, not just one little part of it. That is why you must read, that is why you must look at the skies,

that is why you must sing, and dance, and write poems, and suffer,
and understand, for all that is life."
Jiddu Krishnamurti

"Enlightenment is the ending of suffering."
The Buddha

"There is no path to happiness: happiness is the path."
The Buddha

"You will not be punished for your anger; you will be punished by
your anger."
Buddha

"However many holy words you read, however many you speak,
what good will they do you if you do not act on upon them?"
The Buddha

"The whole secret of existence is to have no fear. Never fear what
will become of you, depend on no one. Only the moment you reject
all help are you freed."
The Buddha

"Doing as others told me, I was blind.
Coming when others called me, I was lost.
Then I left everyone, myself as well.
Then I found everyone, myself as well."
Rumi

"When I am silent,
I have thunder hidden inside."
Rumi

"When you feel a peaceful joy,
that's when you are near truth."
Rumi

"Self-abandonment is the creed and religion of Lovers."
Rumi

"This being human is a guest-house.
Every morning a new arrival.
A joy, a depression, a meanness,
some momentary awareness comes
as an unexpected visitor.
Welcome and entertain them all!
Even if they're a crowd of sorrows,
who violently sweep your house
empty of its furniture.
Still, treat each guest honorably,
who may be clearing you out
for some new delight.
The dark thought, the shame, the malice,
meet them at the door laughing,
and invite them in.
Be grateful for whoever comes,
because each has been sent as a guide from beyond."
Rumi

"I, you, he, she, we
In the garden of mystic lovers,
these are not true distinctions."
Rumi

"If you love only those who love you, what reward will you get? Are
not even the tax collectors doing that?"
Jesus

"For what shall it profit a man, if he shall gain the whole world, and
lose his own soul?"
Jesus

"Let he who is without sin, cast the first stone."
Jesus

"Happiness is the meaning and the purpose of life, the whole aim
and end of human existence."
Aristotle

"Educating the mind without educating the heart is no education at all."
Aristotle

"Knowing yourself is the beginning of all wisdom."
Aristotle

"Whatever one of us blames in another, each one will find in his own heart."
Seneca

"The unexamined life is not worth living."
Socrates

"Contentment is natural wealth, luxury is artificial poverty."
 Socrates

"Difficulties strengthen the mind, as labor does the body."
Seneca

"A person's fears are lighter when the danger is at hand."
Seneca

"Men are disturbed not by things, but by the view which they take of them."
Epictetus

"The energy of the mind is the essence of life."
Aristotle

"Love is composed of a single soul inhabiting two bodies."
Aristotle

"I am not an Athenian, nor a Greek, but a citizen of the world."
Socrates

"He is rich who is content with the least; for contentment is the wealth of nature."
 Socrates

"The only true wisdom is in knowing you know nothing."
Socrates

"As death, when we come to consider it closely, is the true goal of our existence, I have formed during the last few years such close relationships with this best and truest friend of mankind that death's image is not only no longer terrifying to me, but is indeed very soothing and consoling."
Mozart

"The best and most beautiful things in the world cannot be seen or even touched. They must be felt with the heart."
Helen Keller

"You change your life by changing your heart."
Max Lucado

"The pessimist complains about the wind; the optimist expects it to change; the realist adjusts the sails."
William Arthur Ward

"The greatest obstacle to discovery is not ignorance - it is the illusion of knowledge."
Daniel J. Boorstin

"Never does nature say one thing and wisdom another."
Juvenal

"We don't stop playing because we grow old; we grow old because we stop playing."
George Bernard Shaw

"Age is an issue of mind over matter. If you don't mind, it doesn't matter."
Mark Twain

"Life's tragedy is that we get old too soon and wise too late."
Benjamin Franklin

"Beauty is in the eye of the beholder."
Margaret Hungerford

"Some people, no matter how old they get, never lose their beauty – they merely move it from their faces into their hearts."
Martin Buxbaum

"It is not beauty that endears; it's love that makes us see beauty."
Leo Tolstoy

"The only thing constant in life is change."
Francois de la Rochefoucauld

"As a well-spent day brings happy sleep, so a life well spent brings happy death."
Leonardo da Vinci

"Happiness is a butterfly which, when pursued, is always just beyond your grasp but which, if you will sit down quietly, may alight upon you."
Nathaniel Hawthorne

"Whenever I climb I am followed by a dog called 'Ego'."
Friedrich Nietzsche

"The instinct of nearly all societies is to lock up anybody who is truly free. First, society begins by trying to beat you up. If this fails, they try to poison you. If this fails too, they finish by loading honors on your head."
Jean Cocteau

"God, please save me from your followers!"
Bumper Sticker

"My advice to you is get married: if you find a good wife you'll be happy; if not, you'll become a philosopher."
Socrates

"Wise men make proverbs, but fools repeat them."
Samuel Palmer

"The price of anything is the amount of life you exchange for it."
Henry David Thoreau

"The greatness of a nation and its moral progress can be judged by the way its animals are treated."
Mahatma Gandhi

"Simplicity is the ultimate sophistication."
Leonardo da Vinci

"How we spend our days is, of course, how we spend our lives."
Annie Dillard

"Try not to become a man of success, but rather try to become a man of value." Albert Einstein

"Destroying rain forest for economic gain is like burning a Renaissance painting to cook a meal."
Edward O. Wilson

"It is pleasant to have been to a place the way a river went."
Thoreau

"One of the first conditions of happiness is that the link between Man and Nature shall not be broken."
Leo Tolstoy

"I always wondered why somebody doesn't do something about that. Then I realized I was somebody."
Lily Tomlin

"We need to find God, and he cannot be found in noise and restlessness. God is the friend of silence. See how nature, trees, flowers, grass grows in silence; see the stars, the moon and the sun, how they move in silence. We need silence to be able to touch souls."
Mother Teresa

"To me, wholeness is the key to aliveness. It is more than just physical vitality; it is radiance, coming from being at one with yourself and your experience. Life then flows through you."
 Richard Moss

"When the heart grieves over what it has lost, the spirit rejoices over what it has left."
Sufi saying

"There is no way to peace. Peace is the way."
 Unknown

"You cannot discover oceans unless you have the courage to leave the shore." Unknown

"The happiest of people don't necessarily have the best of everything; they just make the most of everything that comes along their way."
 Karen S. Magee

"Live one day at a time and make it a masterpiece."
Dale West

"Do not go where the path may lead, go instead where there is no path and leave a trail."
Ralph Waldo Emerson

"Happiness is a journey, not a destination. For a long time it seemed to me that life was about to begin - real life. But there was always some obstacle in the way, something to be gotten through first, some unfinished business, time still to be served, a debt to be paid. At last it dawned on me that these obstacles were my life. This perspective has helped me to see there is no way to happiness. Happiness is the way. So treasure every moment you have and remember that time waits for no one."
Souza

"I'm convinced that the only thing that kept me going was that I loved what I did. You've got to find what you love. And that is as true for your work as it is for your lovers. Your work is going to fill a

large part of your life, and the only way to be truly satisfied is to do what you believe is great work. And the only way to do great work is to love what you do. If you haven't found it yet, keep looking. Don't settle. As with all matters of the heart, you'll know when you find it. And, like any great relationship, it just gets better and better as the years roll on. So keep looking until you find it. Don't settle."
Steve Jobs

"If we listened to our intellect, we'd never have a love affair. We'd never have a friendship. We'd never go into business, because we'd be too cynical. Well, that's nonsense. You've got to jump off cliffs all the time and build your wings on the way down."
Annie Dillard

"It is not what we take up, but what we give up, that makes us rich."
Henry Ward Beecher

"If you are filled with pride, then you will have no room for wisdom."
African proverb

"Make some money but don't let money make you."
African proverb

"Anyone who sees beauty and does not look at it will soon be poor."
Yoruba Proverb

"If there is character, ugliness becomes beauty; if there is none, beauty becomes ugliness."
Nigerian Proverb

"The real voyage of discovery consists not in seeking new lands but seeing with new eyes."
Marcel Proust

"If you want to tell people the truth, make them laugh, otherwise they'll kill you."
Oscar Wilde

"Perfection is achieved, not when there is nothing more to add, but when there is nothing left to take away."
Antoine de Saint-Exupéry

"The richest man is not he who has the most, but he who needs the least."
Unknown

"When hungry, eat your rice; when tired, close your eyes. Fools may laugh at me, but wise men will know what I mean."
Lin-Chi

"Never mistake knowledge for wisdom. One helps you make a living; the other helps you make a life."
Sandra Carey

"Your time is limited, so don't waste it living someone else's life. Don't be trapped by dogma which is living with the results of other people's thinking. Don't let the noise of others' opinions drown out your own inner voice. And most importantly, have the courage to follow your heart and intuition. They somehow already know what you truly want to become. Everything else is secondary."
Steve Jobs

"Remembering you are going to die is the best way I know to avoid the trap of thinking you have something to lose. You are already naked. There is no reason not to follow your heart."
Steve Jobs

"Don't ask yourself what the world needs, ask yourself what makes you come alive. And then go and do that. Because what the world needs is people who are alive."
Howard Thurman

"A bird doesn't sing because it has an answer, it sings because it has a song."
Maya Angelou

"Do not pity the dead, Harry. Pity the living, and, above all those who live without love."
J.K. Rowling

"I wanted a perfect ending. Now I've learned, the hard way, that some poems don't rhyme, and some stories don't have a clear beginning, middle, and end. Life is about not knowing, having to change, taking the moment and making the best of it, without knowing what's going to happen next. Delicious Ambiguity."
Gilda Radner

"I speak to everyone in the same way, whether he is the garbage man or the president of the university."
Albert Einstein

"If A is a success in life, then A equals x plus y plus z. Work is x; y is play; and z is keeping your mouth shut."
Albert Einstein

"A human being is a part of the whole called by us universe, a part limited in time and space. He experiences himself, his thoughts and feeling as something separated from the rest, a kind of optical delusion of his consciousness. This delusion is a kind of prison for us, restricting us to our personal desires and to affection for a few persons nearest to us. Our task must be to free ourselves from this prison by widening our circle of compassion to embrace all living creatures and the whole of nature in its beauty."
Albert Einstein

"The real lover is the man who can thrill you by kissing your forehead or smiling into your eyes or just staring into space."
Marilyn Monroe

"Listen to the mustn'ts, child. Listen to the don'ts. Listen to the shouldn'ts, the impossibles, the won'ts. Listen to the never haves, then listen close to me... Anything can happen, child. Anything can be."
Shel Silverstein

"Choose a job you love, and you will never have to work a day in your life."
Confucius

"I am nothing special, of this I am sure. I am a common man with common thoughts and I've led a common life. There are no monuments dedicated to me and my name will soon be forgotten, but I've loved another with all my heart and soul, and to me, this has always been enough."
Nicholas Sparks

"I sought to hear the voice of God and climbed the topmost steeple, but God declared: 'Go down again! I dwell among the people.'"
John Henry Newman

"Animals are my friends, and I don't eat my friends."
George Bernard Shaw

"I would believe only in a God that knows how to dance."
Friedrich Nietzsche

"The individual has always had to struggle to keep from being overwhelmed by the tribe. If you try it, you will be lonely often, and sometimes frightened. But no price is too high to pay for the privilege of owning yourself."
Friedrich Nietzsche

"Sometimes people don't want to hear the truth because they don't want their illusions destroyed."
Friedrich Nietzsche

"In individuals, insanity is rare; but in groups, parties, nations and epochs, it is the rule."
Friedrich Nietzsche

"Look for God. Look for God like a man with his head on fire looks for water."
Elizabeth Gilbert

"There are people in the world so hungry, that God cannot appear to them except in the form of bread."
Mahatma Gandhi

"Nothing is impossible, the word itself says 'I'm possible'!"
Audrey Hepburn

"I love people who make me laugh. I honestly think it's the thing I like most, to laugh. It cures a multitude of ills. It's probably the most important thing in a person."
Audrey Hepburn

"The beauty of a woman is not in the clothes she wears, the figure that she carries, or the way she combs her hair. The beauty of a woman is seen in her eyes, because that is the doorway to her heart, the place where love resides. True beauty in a woman is reflected in her soul. It's the caring that she lovingly gives, the passion that she shows and the beauty of a woman only grows with passing years."
Audrey Hepburn

"I was born with an enormous need for affection, and a terrible need to give it."
Audrey Hepburn

"You can tell more about a person by what he says about others than you can by what others say about him."
Audrey Hepburn

"The gratification comes in the doing, not in the results."
James Dean

"When I had nothing to lose, I had everything. When I stopped being who I am, I found myself."
Paulo Coelho

"Tell your heart that the fear of suffering is worse than the suffering itself."
Paulo Coelho

"Seems to me it ain't the world that's so bad but what we're doing to it, and all I'm saying is: see what a wonderful world it would be if only we'd give it a chance. Love, baby - love. That's the secret."
Louis Armstrong

"Success is not the key to happiness. Happiness is the key to success. If you love what you are doing, you will be successful."
Schweitzer

"Live each day like it's your last, cause one day you gonna be right."
Ray Charles

"I've always found that the most beautiful people, truly beautiful inside and out, are the ones who are quietly unaware of their effect."
 Jennifer L. Armentrout

"The saddest aspect of life right now is that science gathers knowledge faster than society gathers wisdom."
Isaac Asimov

"Peace. It does not mean to be in a place where there is no noise, trouble or hard work. It means to be in the midst of those things and still be calm in your heart."
Unknown

"The fear of death follows from the fear of life. A man who lives fully is prepared to die at any time."
Mark Twain

"Some people feel the rain. Others just get wet."
Bob Marley

"Don't gain the world and lose your soul. Wisdom Is better than silver or gold."
Bob Marley

"If you judge people, you have no time to love them."
Mother Teresa

"I am not sure exactly what heaven will be like, but I know that when we die and it comes time for God to judge us, he will not ask, 'How many good things have you done in your life?' rather he will ask, 'How much love did you put into what you did?'"
Mother Teresa

"Not all of us can do great things. But we can do small things with great love."
Mother Teresa

"When I was 5 years old, my mother always told me that happiness was the key to life. When I went to school, they asked me what I wanted to be when I grew up. I wrote down 'happy'. They told me I didn't understand the assignment, and I told them they didn't understand life."
John Lennon

"When one door of happiness closes, another opens; but often we look so long at the closed door that we do not see the one which has been opened for us."
Helen Keller

"Everyone thinks of changing the world, but no one thinks of changing himself."
Leo Tolstoy

"If you tell the truth, you don't have to remember anything."
Mark Twain

"Life is what happens to you while you're busy making other plans."
John Lennon

"Don't walk behind me; I may not lead. Don't walk in front of me; I may not follow. Just walk beside me and be my friend."
Albert Camus

"A woman's heart should be so hidden in God that a man has to seek Him just to find her."
Maya Angelou

NATIVE AMERICAN QUOTES

"Before our white brothers came to civilize us we had no jails. Therefore we had no criminals. You can't have criminals without a jail. We had no locks or keys, and so we had no thieves. If someone was so poor that he had no horse, tipi or blanket, someone gave him these things. We were too uncivilized to set much value on personal belongings. We wanted to have things only in order to give them away. We had no money, and therefore a man's worth couldn't be measured by it. We had no written law, no attorneys or politicians, therefore we couldn't cheat. We really were in a bad way before the white men came, and I don't know how we managed to get along without these basic things which, we are told, are absolutely necessary to make a civilized society."
John (Fire) Lame Deer

"Love is something you and I must have. We must have it because our spirit feeds upon it. We must have it because without it we become weak and faint. Without love our self-esteem weakens. Without it our courage fails. Without love we can no longer look out confidently at the world. We turn inward and begin to feed upon our own personalities, and little by little we destroy ourselves. With it, we are creative. With it, we march tirelessly. With it, and with it alone, we are able to sacrifice for others." Chief Dan George

"Knowledge was inherent in all things. The world was a library and its books were the stones, leaves, grass, brooks and the birds and animals that shared, alike with us, the storms and blessings of the earth. We learn to do what only the student of nature ever learns, and that is to feel beauty. We never rail at the storms, the furious winds, the biting frosts and snows. To do so intensifies human futility, so whatever comes we should adjust ourselves by more effort and energy if necessary, but without complaint. Bright days and dark days are both expressions of the Great Mystery, and the Indian reveled in being close the Great Holiness."
Chief Luther Standing Bear

"Only when the last tree has died and the last river been poisoned and the last fish been caught will we realize we cannot eat money."
Cree Indian Proverb

"By awakening the Native American teachings, you come to the realization that the earth is not something simply that you build upon and walk upon and drive upon and take for granted. It is a living entity. It has consciousness."
Edgar Cayce

"The earth is the mother of all people, and all people should have equal rights upon it."
Chief Joseph

"It does not require many words to speak the truth."
Chief Joseph

"Some day the earth will weep, she will beg for her life, she will cry with tears of blood. You will make a choice, if you will help her or let her die, and when she dies, you too will die."
John Hollow Horn, Oglala Lakota

"Their motto seems to be 'Money, money, get money, get rich, and be a gentleman.' With this sentiment, they fly about in every direction, like a swarm of bees, in search of treasure that lies so near to their hearts."
Kahkewaquonaby, Ojibwe

"The Elders say the men should look at women in a sacred way. The men should never put women down or shame them in any way. When we have problems, we should seek their counsel. We should share with them openly. A woman has intuitive thought. She has access to another system of knowledge that few men develop. She can help us understand. We must treat her in a good way."
Anonymous

"May the sun bring you new energy by day, may the moon softly restore you by night, may the rain wash away your worries, may the breeze blow new strength into your being, may you walk gently through the world and know its beauty all the days of your life."
Apache blessing

Ancient Wisdom In Modern Times

Ancient wisdom says, if genuine jade is made in the secret gardens of love, it will connect one to "qi", the universal energy which guides to the true path of fortune, prosperity, peace and happiness.

SENZANOME

The Jade Coin Collections

Become a Citizen of the Prosperous Kingdom

www.senzanome.com

Made in the USA
Lexington, KY
19 December 2019